Playing Big

The Unsexy Truth
About How To Succeed In Business

Kim Flynn

Published by Big Wake Publishing
51 W. Center St. #310
Orem UT 84057

All client stories in this book are based on real people, however, names and situations have been changed to protect their identity.

Order Additional Copies at www.KimFlynn.com

Special discounts are available on quantity purchases by corporations, associations, and others. For details, contact our office at the address above.

Playing Big: The Unsexy Truth About How To Succeed In Business/ Kim Flynn. -- 1st ed.

ISBN 978-0-9915049-0-9

This book is dedicated to my sweetheart.
It takes a lot of patience to be married to an entrepreneur,
and you have mastered that skill.
Love you always.

TABLE OF CONTENTS

FOREWORD

I am not a motivational speaker and this is not a motivational book. As much as other books, coaches, motivational speakers, and celebrity business owners can make growing a business seem thrilling, larger-than-life and full of excitement, the behind-the-scenes truth is that business is mostly blood, sweat, and tears. Business is not sexy.

The purpose of this book is not to discourage you from starting a business or growing the one you have. The purpose of this book is to set you up for realistic expectations about what takes to grow your business. In business, as long as you get the training you need, have a solid business plan, and keep putting one foot in front of the other, there is a good chance you will have success. Business owners often don't see success because they get impatient and they quit. They quit because they expect building a business to be sexy.

> I am not a motivational speaker and this is not a motivational book.

If you can go into business knowing that it will be hard, wili take longer than you think, and will take more money than you expected, you will have the courage and the stamina to keep going, month after month, year after year, until you reach your destination.

Because of its difficult nature, business is the best personal development program ever developed. While the ride won't be glamorous, it will be fulfilling. You will meet every weakness you didn't know you had. You will accomplish hard things you never knew you could. You will learn things you didn't even know you didn't know. You will emerge a different person than the person you are now; a stronger, more resilient, more skilled, and yes, probably a little more calloused, version of you. Building a business is not for the faint of heart, but if you can keep putting one foot in front of the other amid the hard times, you will reach the other side a more influential person and a much more capable leader than you are today.

And isn't that what it is all about? Isn't building a business about more than getting money and retiring to an island in isolation? Building a business means becoming a mover and a shaker. It means that when you see a problem, and maybe you see a HUGE problem like poverty in America, hunger in the Sudan, sex trafficking in Asia, the prison system mess, Malaria in Nigeria, illiteracy or any other problem that speaks to your heart, you have the financial resources, the leadership skills, and the circle of influence to help alleviate some of the world's pain. Training you to become that person is my "why".

I don't want to motivate you with pictures of Lear jets and Lamborghinis and Caribbean islands. I want you to feel the calling to literally change your piece of the world. I want you to gain the skills both personally and professionally so when you see a problem that calls to you, you will have the skill set and resources to become a part of the solution.

I am calling leaders. Not as you are--with self-doubt and inexperience. But as you will be. I am calling you to learn to do hard things, to learn how to lead, how to organize resources and solve problems, so that when you meet the purpose of your life, you will not shrink from the challenge. I am calling you to take the first step to becoming that person.

This book is a preparation and guide book for that journey. Unfortunately for us all, this book isn't sexy either. This is a nuts and bolts guide to exactly what you will need to know, personally and in your business, to begin to build a successful business.

The first section will introduce to you realistic expectations of what it takes to build a business. This section will not give you warm fuzzies, will not induce strong desires in you to stand up and cheer, and will probably even discourage you from going into business if you are on the fence. At the same time, this book will also give you realistic expectations of what your experience will be like, when to expect money to come in, and how exactly to take the big dream in your heart and make that a reality.

> I am calling leaders. Not as you are – with self-doubt and inexperience. But as you will be. I am calling you to learn to do hard things, to learn how to lead, how to organize resources and solve problems.

The next section of this book will ask you to evaluate your business as it stands now. You will determine exactly where you are in business (and often that is at point A even if you have been in business for years). I will then ask you what your BIG dreams are, and why those are your dreams. We want to make sure that you are chasing YOUR dreams and not someone else's. Next comes the magic of this section; you will create a step-by-step plan to get from where you are now to where you want to be. That is the fun part for me, and might be the really challenging part for you. It forces you to begin taking action, even when it is scary.

After that, we move into what I call the "eat your broccoli" content. You know it is good for you and you know your business needs it, but it might not be as fun to consume as the more self-evaluative content in the first two sections. It is the unsexy nuts and bolts of a business: your business structure.

We will go through all five parts of a business (leadership, customer service/fulfillment, finance/accounting, product, and marketing/sales) and discuss how to structure and organize each of these categories. I will ask you to evaluate where you are in your business, and give you a plan to implement the training in your business. The business strategies you will learn in this book will probably take a year to implement. That may sound like an eternity in a world of "7 Steps to Becoming a Millionaire Next Week" but trust me on this one. It will probably take you at least a year. Be patient with the process. You are building a solid business--not a get-rich-quick scheme.

If you are committed to building your business, you will survive Playing Big in Finance of this book and move onto the next section, Playing Big in Marketing. I won't have any way of knowing this, but I am guessing that 90% of the people who read this book won't get past this section. I dare you to get through all of it! It will be another drink-from-the-fire-hose experience. You will learn the comprehensive SELL SUM marketing system. You will know exactly where the holes are in your current marketing program, and you will know what you need to do to fill those holes.

And just when your brain is tired and your circuits are blown, I will lead you back to your big WHY in the last chapter. We will explore what it is like to be successful in business, why it is that you are called to build a business, and how you can use the skills and resources gained to do something extraordinary in your life. We will take you back to your ultimate purpose of building your business, which is gaining skills and leadership so that you can have an influence for good in the world.

I love the scripture in the Bible in Matthew 24:14 "Many are called, but few are chosen." If you are reading this book, you have been called to grow your business. You have been called because you can feel it in your chest - a desire, or a pull towards business. I believe that if you feel that pull within you, that pull was put there by the God that created you. You have been called.

The "few are chosen" part of this scripture is up to you. Will you have the strength and the courage to keep putting one foot in front of the other, even when things are hard, to grow your business? Will you do the hard things, like implementing the strategies you will learn in this book and educating yourself in areas where you are weak, even if it isn't fun? Will you be one of the few that are chosen? You get to choose.

CHAPTER 1

MOTIVATIONAL MYTHS THAT WILL PREVENT YOU FROM PLAYING BIG

I recently hosted an internet marketing training seminar and wanted to conduct an experiment. I intentionally invited a mix of experts to speak. In my opening remarks before the first speaker started, I challenged the audience to be discerning.

I spoke into the microphone. "There are generally two types of business speakers in the world. Those who do; these are the guys in their boxer shorts 'til two in the morning on their computers. They may not be the most engaging speakers, and your heart will *not* burn inside of you when you hear them speak, but they will teach you what actually works. They know their stuff."

I continued, "Then there are those who have a speaking gift. These are the speakers that *will* make your heart burn inside with inspiration and good feelings. They have a gift of engaging you, and you will want to believe and follow every word they say. The problem is, best case scenario, they get you inspired but you have no action steps to take. Worst case scenario, they don't know what they are talking about and they can give very bad advice. They often speak about what I call Motivational Myths: principles that sound great from the stage, but don't apply to the reality of building a business."

I continued, "In an ideal world, those who have a speaking gift will constantly be learning from the doers so their content is accurate."

> Building a business is not entertaining. Building a business is doing those calculated, often boring, steps day after day after day. Business is not sexy.

Then came the challenge. "I am conducting an experiment this weekend. I have intentionally invited both types of speakers to this event. I challenge you to ask yourself, 'Is this a doer, or is this a motivator?' Of course you will enjoy the motivators' presentations, as you should. But being entertained is not how we grow a business. Focus on the doer presentations. Look past their nerdiness, and focus on the how-to's. Building a business is not entertaining. Building a business is doing those calculated, often boring, steps day after day after day. Business is not sexy."

Sure enough, after my warning, the first speaker to step up onto the stage was Warren. He wore khaki pants, and pink shirt, and a matching tie and looked like he was going to church in 1995. He started into his presentation on SEO (search engine optimization) without any stories or fanfare, just giving us the information straight. Warren was an absolute expert in his field. The content he was giving us was relevant, immediately applicable, and important to learn. It was exactly what I wanted to provide for my attendees.

I sat on the side of the room, scanning the people in the audience. A few people seemed to understand the value of the content they were getting; they were busy taking notes and soaking it in.

The majority, however, looked a little bit glassy. Most small business owners attending conferences are used to being inspired and uplifted and emotionally challenged. Warren was doing none of these.

A few presentations later, the speaker I had been anticipating stepped onto the stage. I had invited him for a reason.

Dave walked onto the stage with confidence and a pair of designer jeans. Immediately the entire room woke up. I watched as the entire room leaned forward. All cell phones were ignored. Even note taking was abandoned. The audience laughed when Dave wanted them to laugh. They cried when Dave cried. They went on an inspirational, emotional whirlwind and were entertained and motivated every step of the way. They didn't seem to notice that there was nothing to implement in Dave's presentation.

> Business basics had once again been thwarted by motivational myths. At my own conference.

Before we broke for lunch that first day, I reiterated the challenge. "Pay attention to the speakers who really are experts in their fields. If you feel your emotions going on a roller coaster, you are probably listening to a gifted motivational speaker. You may be inspired by them, but business is not built with motivational myths. I want you to practice discerning between the two."

The conference ended the next day, and I went out to dinner with several of the attendees.

"What was your highlight?" I asked to the group of eight people around the restaurant table.

"Dave was amazing," said the first. "I was just so inspired!"

"Yeah, Dave was definitely my favorite. He made it seem so easy to build a business. I guess I have just been over-thinking it," said the next person.

The third person spoke up, "I love how he made me feel; like I really can do this."

I wanted to cry.

I had intentionally invited Dave to be an obvious juxtaposition to the Warrens of the world; I wanted my audience to realize that they needed accurate information from someone who has expertise, whether or not that knowledge is exciting. I wanted them to see through Dave, and instead appreciate the training they got from the Warrens. They hadn't.

Business basics had once again been thwarted by motivational myths. At my own conference.

There are five motivational myths that are running rampant and spread by the Daves of the entrepreneurial world. These myths are dangerous. For the good of your business I want to dispel these myths one by one.

Motivational Myth #1:
You can attract Business Success from the Universe

In 2006, a film and accompanying book sold 21 million copies and took the thought leadership world by storm. The main idea of the book is if you think positive thoughts, because of the law of attraction, the universe has no choice but to give you what you think about. The principles in the book were widely applied to business, and the attraction teachings have made their way into almost every entrepreneurial summit and business conference in the country.

I have no problem whatsoever with encouraging people to take themselves out of victim mode and think positively. I do have a problem when people expect the law of attraction to grow their business for them.

> I don't believe in the law of attraction because it cheats the law of the harvest, or the law of cost.

Attend any women's entrepreneurial seminar in the country, and you will hear "Vision Boards" talked about, if not actually workshopped at the conference.

To create a vision board, a stack of magazines is provided to the group, and each person flips through them, finding pictures of cars and islands and mansions that resonate with them. The women then make a collage out of the pictures of yachts and cars, and are told that when they hang this poster board on their wall and look at it every day, believing that those things will come to them, the universe will have to comply through the law of attraction and give them what they want. Sadly, this is not how wealth is built.

I don't believe in the law of attraction.

I don't believe in the law of attraction because it cheats the law of the harvest, or the law of cost.

With a few exceptions (winning the lottery), there is a price for everything we gain in our lives. There is a price to pay if you want to be healthy; you must eat nutritious foods and exercise regularly. There is a price to pay if you want a good marriage; you must be kind to your spouse and give the relationship time and attention. There is also a price to pay to earn money in your business; you must acquire knowledge, gain experience, and work hard. If you don't pay the price, you don't earn the reward. And then after the hard work, there is never a guarantee. Life always has permission to throw us curve balls.

I have no problem whatsoever with encouraging people to take themselves out of the victim mode and think positively. I do have a problem when people expect the law of attraction to grow their business for them.

If you don't pay the price to earn money in your business, you will not have the means to buy those cars, islands and mansions you put on your dreamboard. No matter how much you believe, no matter how much you think positively, the law of the harvest still applies. It is fun to dream that you will win the lottery, but only one person in 75,000,000 will actually do that. Your odds of having the universe deliver you a car, an island, or a mansion without your paying the price to earn those results is just as remote.

The unsexy truth is you will have to work for everything you gain. If you can channel the time you spend dreaming about your goals and attending motivational conferences and put that time into applying and implementing the nuts and bolts strategies that you will read about in this book, you will start to see successes. You will be on your way to operating and sustaining a successful small business so you can afford to purchase the island vacations and nice car. While working hard for ten years isn't as thrilling as putting pictures on poster board and waiting for a hand-out, it is more realistic.

Motivational Myth #2
You Can Shortcut Growth if You Have Talent

"If people knew how hard I worked to achieve my mastery, it wouldn't seem so wonderful after all."
-Michelangelo

"Talent is cheaper than table salt. What separates the talented individual from the successful one is a lot of hard work." -Stephen King

> What you need to ask yourself is, 'Am I committed to my business education?' "

You have probably heard of the 10,000 hour rule. This rule, made popular by Malcolm Gladwell's book *Outliers*, proposes that it takes about 10,000 hours to master just about anything. That means that if you work at something for three hours a day it will take you about ten years to master it, and if you work at something full time you will master it in about five.

How do we apply this to business?

The first step to apply this in your life is to hose down those dreams in the sky that you will have instant success. Even if you are unbelievably talented. Even if your idea is the BEST idea ever. Even if you already have funding. Even if you are working with the stars from the Shark Tank. Even if you need money now. Even if your best friend thinks you are the best entrepreneur ever.

I consider those 10,000 hours your business education. They are essential.

My client Susan struggles with the Instant Success Syndrome. Susan has a natural business talent and works hard. She was building a seminar and workshop business from the ground up, with no previous business experience. Her dream was to create an international organization for teens.

After working on her business for about six months, and after hosting her first workshop, she prematurely rented $6000 in event space and was struggling to fill seats with paying clients. She called me in tears. She had not yet seen any money coming in, and was doubting herself and the business education process.

She asked me, "How long did it take you to start making money in your business?"

And I told her, "You are asking the wrong question. What you need to ask yourself is, 'Am I committed to my business education?' "When you are committed to your education, you stop asking yourself "When?" and start asking yourself, "What is my next step?" You don't expect it to come easy; you are committed to taking action every day for an indefinite, undetermined amount of time; even if that is more than 10,000 hours. There is no time limit when you say to yourself, "I'll just try for x amount of time. If I haven't made it by then, I can quit." You are undermining your chances of success when you say to yourself, "I'll just put myself out there a little bit. When it starts to get hard, I can quit."

Entrepreneurs commonly use a time limit to keep themselves motivated. They tell themselves, "I will work really hard for a year, and surely I will be making money by then." The year comes and goes, and when they are still putting more money into their businesses than they are taking out they deem themselves failures and quit. This is understandable human nature, but you will have to adopt a different way of motivating yourself to be successful in business.

> This is understandable human nature, but you will have to adopt a different way of motivating yourself to be successful in business.

Your motivation will need to be internal. Your business *"why"* is what pulls you on even when things get hard. Why are you going into business in the first place? Your *why* will need to be compelling, inspiring, and rock-solid. Do you know in your heart that you have a purpose and a mission here on earth, and your business is part of that purpose? If you can feel that calling from within, and know that it has been put there by the God that created you, you will be able to keep putting one foot in front of the other, every day, for as long as it takes. You are committed to your education.

Here are some questions to get you thinking about your *why*. It is already inside of you (or else you wouldn't be reading this book), but may need some teasing to come out. These questions serve as a jumping off point to explore what your subconscious mind already knows. Take five minutes to answer the questions below, writing as much as you can; no editing. If you find yourself thinking, "That would be arrogant of me to admit," or "I could never do that," gently dismiss those thoughts and keep writing. The questions may seem unrelated, but they will help you pull out your values, priorities and your *why* for business.

Be honest with yourself as you write. If you don't feel a pull to help cure cancer, don't feel compelled to put it down.

- When/what was your first entrepreneurial experience? How did you feel?

- What life experiences have you had that pull you toward your business?

- If you had 50 million dollars to spend every month, what would you do with it?

- If you knew you could not fail, what would you do?

As soon as I asked my client Susan about her *why*, she recommitted to her education. "I know I am supposed to be helping these girls. I am absolutely committed to building this business for however long it takes." She stopped looking for instant success, and stopped looking at setbacks and difficulties as reasons to quit, and instead looked at them as challenges to gain her education. Ironically, she is also less frantic and lets herself take breaks. She knows she will be working at this for the next ten years, and doesn't feel compelled to be an instant success tomorrow. She is committed to her education.

The Woodcarver Principle

In my house growing up, we had large two-foot-tall wood carvings of the famous fictional characters Don Quixote and Sancho, his side kick. They were intricately carved out of dark wood, and I remember running my fingers over the figures, fascinated that blocks of wood could come to life through an artist's skill.

The thought of gluing a picture of a wood carving on a dream board and expecting the universe to give you the skills to create that woodcarving seems ludicrous. So does expecting yourself to become a master wood carver in six months.

> Instead of dreaming of instant success, commit to your education. Commit to becoming a master, an aim for steady, slow, long-term business success.

What would it take to become a master woodcarver?

If you were to sit down right now with a block of wood and a carving knife in your hand, without woodcarving experience, and attempt to carve out Don Quixote, your efforts would not produce Don Quixote. You would be an awful wood carver, and your results would reflect that.

But what if you sat down with a block of wood every day, working with a mentor or teacher on a regular basis, and practiced carving that wood day in and day out? You would eventually become a decent woodcarver, and if you continued long enough, even when practicing got tedious and boring and decidedly unsexy, you would become a master woodcarver. And because you took the time to *become*, you would be able to *create* a master woodcarving of Don Quixote.

That is what you are going to do in your business. Long after the dreams of becoming an instant success have come and gone, you will be putting one foot in front of the other, day in and day out, doing all of the unsexy tasks that you will learn about in this book, and you will *become* a master at business. And then you will be able to *create* a bank account and a degree of influence that comes only through *becoming* first.

Instead of dreaming of instant success, commit to your education. Commit to becoming a master, and aim for steady, slow, long-term business success.

Motivational Myth #3: You Can Shortcut Growth by Using One Amazing Strategy

Ugg. If there is anything that makes me cringe, it is the promise of making millions by just using "this one proven strategy!".

It was August 2010 in Chicago. At the time, I was getting my foot in the door in the platform sales industry, the seminar business model where a series of speakers all sell their product from stage one after another. I was in the back of the room, watching the other speakers work the stage. Trying to improve my own skills, I was paying close attention to each presentation. A well-known speaker was taking the stage.

> You can't shortcut growth no matter how many testimonials you read, how many products you buy, how much money you spend, or how many guarantees are promised.

Jeff looked like a rockstar. He had on snake-skinned boots, stylin' jeans, an embroidered button-down with his sleeves rolled up, and messy-spiked hair that was popular at the time.

Jeff launched into his presentation with amazing energy and a personality that captured the attention of everyone in the room. He was funny, powerful, and very inspiring with a message that everyone, yes, even you, can change your life and be a millionaire. He assured the audience what he presented was a fail-proof business model. According to Jeff, anyone could be a millionaire by next year if they simply followed the simple five steps which included: (1) buy a derelict mansion with no money down, (2) fix it up using other people's money, (3) stage the house to sell using furnishings you borrow from auction houses, (4) sell the house and the furniture and make a million dollars. He made the process so foolproof, that if you paid $5000 to come to his day-long training seminar, he would guarantee that his team would find you a house to buy before you left. He then showed a video of an 85 year-old woman telling the audience how easy it had been for her, and yes, she was now a millionaire.

I had to lift my jaw off the floor as I watched 80% of the room jump out of their seats and rush to the back of the room to purchase said millionaire-creating strategy package. The purchasers were not real estate savvy. They were mostly people in their 50's, who looked like life hadn't been kind to them. They were throwing away money on a magic pill, instead of investing in their growth.

That is the day I realized I hate some things about my industry. That is also the day that I decided that I would always tell the truth. I would tell my clients how hard it was going to be, how long it was going to take, and how unglamourous the path of a small business owner is.

So here is the unsexy truth: **You Can't Shortcut Growth.**

You can't shortcut growth no matter how many testimonials you read, how many products you buy, how much money you spend, or how many guarantees are promised. If you do make money quickly you will have the lottery experience--you won't have the core abilities to know how to manage money, invest money, or keep it coming to you. You won't be able to hold onto that money or make it grow long term.

One of my favorite growth analogies is the caterpillar to butterfly experience. Imagine that you, in your current business state, are a caterpillar. You are plump and green and furry, and you spend your time crawling along the ground, working hard to grow your business. You look up and see beautiful business butterflies flying above you and you think to yourself, "I want to do that! That looks so easy!"

And you continue to crawl on the ground, wondering how they got to grow wings, while your experience is just a bunch of slow crawling. You search for the solution; you attend seminars, read books, and buy millionaire-creating strategy packages that promise you the ability to fly if you just follow five simple steps, but nothing works. You continue to crawl around on your fuzzy green belly.

Then one day you find a real teacher; a butterfly who is willing to share her experience and teach you how she grew wings and became a butterfly. And she tells you the truth. She doesn't promise five simple steps to grow wings, and she doesn't make the process sound exciting. Instead, she tells you the education process will be very difficult, and sometimes painful, and will take longer than you think.

> And so the caterpillar decides to take a risk. A huge, bold breathtaking risk to try something new and stop looking for magic wing-growing fixes.

And so the caterpillar decides to take a risk. A huge, bold, breathtaking risk to try something new, and stop looking for magic wing-growing fixes.

That's when you stop the busy-ness of crawling, and you opt-in to one of the most difficult decisions of your life: are you ready to leave the world you have known, and enter a new mindset? Are you willing to challenge every belief you have about yourself, and everything you thought you knew about business? Are you willing to scrap your current marketing plan, business plan, or even your current business, for something bigger and scarier? If you say yes to these questions, you enter into the Chrysalis Phase as a caterpillar.

If you don't say yes to these questions, there is nothing wrong with you. You aren't bad or evil, you just aren't ready or aren't feelin' it. That is okay!

But let's assume you are ready to take that bold, breathtaking risk. The caterpillar enters the Chrysalis Phase and from the outside, it may look like you are just in a holding pattern. Your business may not change much initially, and may even seem to slow down.

But on the inside, massive changes are taking place. Most people don't think about what happens inside of a chrysalis. From the outside, it seems as if the plump green caterpillar just gets a little skinnier and grows wings. On the inside it is a different story. Every cell of the caterpillar's body is dissolved to be reformed into an entirely different creature. Every cell. If you were to break open a chrysalis, you would find a big mess of goo. That is what the growth experience will feel like to you.

The Chrysalis Phase of business is not a fun place to be. Every weakness you have is exposed and you no longer have the luxury of hiding behind defenses. You are exposed. You see yourself for who you are for perhaps the first time, and the thought of your real potential scares the hell out of you. You realize that you actually can be anything you want to be, and you can do anything you want to do.

When you go through this experience, and you believe in your true potential for the first time in your life, it will scare you.

When I was going through this process, there were some days when I felt so overwhelmed with internal change, so exposed, and so consistently pushing comfort zone barriers that I felt as if I couldn't breathe. My husband would ask me, "What are you overwhelmed about? What is it that you need to get done?"

And I wouldn't be able to answer him. "I don't know. It just feels like the world is closing in."

Looking back, I can see how quickly I was going through growth on the inside. It is no wonder I couldn't breathe--my insides were a pile of goo.

As I take my high-end clients through this process, I warn them of the inevitable break-down they will experience in their education process. The strong-willed, Warrior personalities tell me, "I really don't break down much. I'll be fine." And I just smile.

I worked with a particularly determined client, Liz, who was tempted from the beginning to look for the magic business pill. Liz came from decades of working in the corporate world, and had easily moved up the corporate ladder. She wore beautiful business suits and red lipstick, and had an air of confidence about her.

She was also very tight on money, and because of her success in the corporate world, expected her business to provide money for her immediately. Despite multiple warnings that money was not going to come quickly, inevitably, on the third month in the process I got the text. She was thinking about giving up. Everything in her business and financial life was falling apart around her and she was tempted to retreat back into a caterpillar body. It was just too hard and was taking too long.

I reminded her of what she was doing; her goal was much loftier than finding a quick fix to get money into the bank. She was not on a mission to find the million-dollar-strategy. She had been trying to shortcut the process of becoming a butterfly by gluing wings onto her caterpillar body.

After I pointed out what she was doing, she gave herself to the education process. Over the next few months I was in awe as I watched her *become*. She no longer looked for shortcuts, no longer lamented her financial position, but embraced the Chrysalis Phase. She stopped believing in the third motivational myth that promises a quick fix, and accepted that you can't shortcut growth. Because of her mental shift, she has also been able to accomplish more in her business in the last few months as well. I am always amazed at what happens when people embrace the education process.

MOTIVATIONAL MYTH #4
You Need to Find the Perfect Business for You

If you find yourself with a dreamer personality, you may fall prey to the fourth motivational myth.

I had only worked with Jill for two weeks when she told me she was switching businesses. Jill was a happy, engaged, light-up-the-room kind of personality. She was fun to work with and eagerly completed each homework assignment in my coaching course.

She had been working with her husband on a real estate business, and after hearing everyone else talk about the passion they felt for their particular business, and hearing motivational speakers say that she needed to find her "soul purpose," Jill got a little purpose-envy.

She announced on our next call that she was no longer working with her husband in real estate, but she really felt committed and interested in essential oils. She had already signed up as a rep in an essential oils network marketing business and felt as if she now had her purpose.

I told her I would be happy to support her in this change, but she had to be sure that she would stick with this second venture. I needed her to commit to the process of growing A business. She readily committed and was diligent in applying the training and education to the new essential oils business.

Then we hit the infamous month three, when clients start to doubt themselves, doubt the education process, and get tired of being a pile of goo. They also get tired of putting one foot in front of the other, and miss the excitement of the initial dream stage of the start-up. Jill called me and said she didn't know if essential oils were for her. She liked them, but she didn't know if they were really her purpose. She wanted to look around for another venture that was her perfect fit; her soul purpose.

My advice to her was, and is to all of you, that we don't wait for our purpose to fall into our laps. We don't wait for God to come to us in a dream and tell us in Morgan Freeman's voice, "Here is your purpose." We don't wait for a business idea so wonderful, so perfectly matched to who we are, or so noble a cause that it makes us sigh with inner world peace.

Instead, we start with where we are. We commit to the process of growing one business. One. We recognize that if we have been pulled to business, that learning business may itself be our purpose at that time. If we don't know exactly what the dream business is yet, we start with whatever is in front of us.

Jill could commit to the real estate business or the essential oils business. It really doesn't matter. What matters is that she learns how to build A business. When her dream business comes a-calling, whether two years from now or twenty, she will have the skills, knowledge, and internal expansion that will enable her to take on her purpose. If she jumps from one business to another, constantly looking for the perfect business, she will miss out on learning how to take a business from point A to point Z.

> Your first business is rarely the dream in the sky. Consider your first business as just practice.

Jill got a lecture from me that sounded like the paragraph you just read. She recommitted herself to the oils business, knowing that it might not be the perfect business for her, but it didn't really matter. She was getting her business education. Jill learned the unsexy truth about business: You won't be able to have influence in your area of purpose if you don't get started with what is in front of you now. Jill was one of the fortunate ones. She realized that the education process was the goal.

Your first business is rarely the dream in the sky. Consider your first business as just practice.

I had another client who didn't learn this, and it was painful to watch. Brynn is one of the most talented people I know. She has the kind of even-keel, grounded personality that makes everyone feel comfortable around her. She has started six businesses, all of which have had the potential of growing from point A to point Z. She started an interior design business, then switched to a mom blog, re-routed to a life coaching business, scrapped them all to start a marketing business, and I just read on her new photography blog that she believes she has now found her purpose.

The tragedy in Brynn's business life is that she has only taken her many start-ups from a point A to a point B. She doesn't have the skills to grow a business beyond that. It isn't because she doesn't have the potential, it is just because she hasn't done it yet. She has spent years of her life taking six different businesses from point A to point B, when she could have taken that first business from point A to point Z. She could be established in her industry; she could be making real money; she could be at a point where she is ready to sell her first business, and move on to the second on financially healthy ground.

Instead, she is still at point A in her sixth business.

At her heart, Brynn is a healer. She has a huge heart, and really wants to help people and influence the world for good. How much influence does she have with a business at point A? She has a small following, and a small amount of money.

If she had stuck with her first business (or even the second or third), she would have a bigger following, and more money to do bigger things. If she is looking for social change and to do good in the world, she is preventing herself from having much influence because of the constant change in businesses. It is hard to see someone with so much potential continue to play in hobby businesses instead of play big in one influential way. Brynn had unfortunately bought in to the motivational myth that you must find the perfect business for you.

MOTIVATIONAL MYTH #5
You Can Quickly Make Money in an MLM

I sigh heavily when I think about network marketing or multi-level marketing (MLM) businesses. It isn't because I don't like the MLM model, it is just frequently misrepresented. The industry is fantastic at promoting the business model as an easy and fast way to make money and have "residual income" to ensure that you won't work for the rest of your life. Please apply the common sense rule when thinking about joining an MLM: just like in a traditional business you will need to work very, very hard to be successful. There is a very, very slim chance that you will find growing your downline to be easy.

That said, there are some people who do really well in the MLM business model.

The people who do well in an MLM are usually one of four types: career builders, zealots, lucky ones and the steady ones.

The first type are career builders, who are usually experienced, charismatic leaders. They are quintessential salespeople. They can sell anything to anyone, and focus on selling the opportunity of making money to others rather than selling the product itself. They are able to build a following of people and sometimes move that following from one MLM business to another. They may also move the following from another type of business over to an MLM. They are powerful and influential leaders, and would probably be successful in any business (or political office) they chose to pursue.

The reason the MLM model works well for them is the business framework is already set up. They don't have to spend their time creating product, managing staff, or worrying about business finances. They can spend all of their time doing what they do best: influencing people (ie selling). If you find yourself resonating with this description, you would probably be a great fit for an MLM.

The people who do well in an MLM are usually one of four types: career builders, zealots, lucky ones and the steady ones.

The second highly successful MLM candidate is the zealot. All members of an MLM are pleased with the product, but all are not zealots. Don't let the word turn you off; it is accurate in describing the almost religious fervor that makes this type of person successful in an MLM setting. Zealots believe strongly in the product, almost to the point of a religious attachment. They will frequently share their testimonies or conversions to the product and how it changed their lives. They are successful because their absolute conviction instills faith in the product in those around them. The belief in the product drives them to continue putting one foot in front of the other, even when things get hard. If you are an avid believer and user of an MLM product and are willing to share that conversion story with those around you, you might be a good candidate to grow an MLM business.

The third type of successful MLM leaders are the steady ones. They achieve success by slowly attracting heavy-hitters onto their downlines who carry them.

The steady ones don't have to be extremely talented as sales people and may not be zealots about the product. These people are just the average network marketing Janes, who work hard enough and long enough to attract some heavy hitters onto their team. They are able to recruit some career builders, and they are able to ride the wave of other's sales skills. I'm not discounting their efforts at all in saying this. It takes plenty of hard work to recruit those builders!

The fourth type of successful MLM leader are the lucky ones. You can get lucky if you time your entrance and exit from an MLM business perfectly. Without your business education, getting lucky is exactly that. Your luck will eventually run out.

Jana was a soft and sweet Mormon homeschooling mom. Her family had moved into a 12,000 square foot home in the prestigious Alpine hills when her chocolate MLM business took off. Jana had gotten into the networking marketing company on the coveted "ground floor." She signed onto the chocolate business when it was exploding in popularity. When the $20,000 monthly checks started coming in, she purchased her dream home. Six months after their family moved in, the checks started dropping. Month after month they watched as the checks went from $15,000 to $5,000 all the way down to $500 per month. The bank foreclosed on their home and they walked away with a great lesson.

I recommend an MLM if . . .

1. You are willing to work hard for a long time
2. You are naturally gifted at influencing (i.e.; selling)
3. You don't want to come up with your own product

If you aren't a born leader or a zealot, and aren't willing to put in the time of a steady one, your success in an MLM might depend on navigating the timing of your entrance and exit strategically. There is nothing wrong with the lucky one strategy; it can work for you if you can ride the wave of a successful MLM, and get off the wave before it crashes. When you get lucky, and those $20,000 monthly checks start coming in the mail, I would ask that you understand that you are using borrowed wings. Please don't count on the money as long-term, or expect it to carry you into retirement. Use it for what it is: a lottery win! Buy a boat, buy a new car with cash, but please don't move into an expensive lifestyle without growing your own wings.

Now let's put an MLM motivational myth to rest. I hear from my clients sometimes that they want to put their real dream on hold so they can quickly make money in an MLM business to fund their dream. Every time I hear it I have to stop myself from choking.

People who create a successful MLM downline work their tails off. I have clients who have been successful in several different MLM's and they have one thing in common; they work really hard for a long time.

When you work really hard for long enough, in the MLM model, you will then be able to work less hard as your downline carries the load.

It sounds a lot like building a regular business; you work really hard getting the business model up and profitable, then you systematize the work to let your employees carry the load.

If you have a big dream (and you have already determined feasibility and researched your market), don't you dare put the dream on the back burner because you think the MLM will be faster. If you put as much effort into your big dream as put into the MLM, you will see results in your business as well. Resist the temptation to believe in someone else's business more than you believe in your own.

I recommend an MLM if . . .
1. You are willing to work hard for a long time
2. You are naturally gifted at influencing (ie selling)
3. You don't want to come up with your own product

If you fit that description, the MLM business model might be a great fit for you, but don't you dare think that easy money will fall from the sky.

Motivational Myth #6
You Need to Get a Big Loan to Start Your Business

Do you want to hear a statistic that has always bothered me?
According to the 2012 US Census Bureau, 1.8% of women-owned businesses reach the million dollar mark, while 5.4% of their male counterparts reach the 7-figure goal. In case you missed that, there is a 300% better chance that a male-owned business will reach the million dollar mark. A little depressing, eh?

One of the main culprits of women playing small in business points back to lack of funding. Only 29% of women owned businesses seek business funding while 71% of their male counterparts do the same.

So why am I telling you that the need to invest big in your business is a myth?

My client Debbie wondered the same thing.

Debbie was at her second Business Intensive Retreat, and was an elite client of mine as well. She had launched her business just a few months before, an internet health training program, and wanted to start a national health competition as her ultimate dream. After hosting her first health workshop (which was a resounding, although expensive success) she felt ready to begin to launch her health competition nationally.

Debbie was usually outspoken and eager to participate in discussions, but that day she hid in the back of the room on a couch, a blanket pulled up to her chin. Even in the back of the room I could tell she was on the verge of tears.

When I had a break in training I asked her what was up.

"I know exactly what I need to do. I know what marketing I need. I have my programs all planned out. The only thing I need is money. That is the only thing that is holding me back."

I hear this from time to time, and I paused to look squarely at her before I launched into the lecture.

"Nope, that's not what you need," I replied. "You need to find out how to get your business model to work systematically, and then you apply funding to grow something that is already working. If you got funding at this point in your business it would be one of the biggest mistakes you could make. You still need to learn the same lessons, you need to learn the same skills, playing with $100 as you would if you had $50,000."

I continued, "After the end of a year in business, the difference in the two scenarios would be $50,000 in debt. You would have the same business experience under your belt. Learn how to run your business with what you have, then after you have proof of concept, then go get funding."

She chose to believe me. She stopped looking for funding, and spent her time working out the kinks in her business model instead.

Nine months later she brought up that conversation again. "Do you remember how I was desperate for funding all those months ago?" she asked.

Of course I remembered.

> The beginning of the business is not when you bring in investors. The unsexy truth is no one should give money to you at this stage.

"I am so glad that I didn't invest lots of money when I started my business! I have changed so much about my business since then. The model I was working on didn't make sense financially, and it isn't even what I want to do now. I am so glad I didn't invest until I figured things out!"

It is so tempting to think, "If I just had $50,000 to play with, I would be able to really get this business off the ground." The myth that you need to invest big in your business to start is just that; a myth.

The beginning of the business is not when you bring in investors. The unsexy truth is no one should give money to you at this stage. You haven't earned anyone's trust. Your business may look good on paper but it is just a gamble until you have proven it with numbers.

Start looking for money when you are two or three years in, have already seen some success, have ironed out the kinks in the system, have predictable numbers (this marketing method equals this many leads, equals this many sales, to pay for this product, that you can provide for this price) and you are ready to take your business to the next level.

Motivational Myth #7

You Can Hire Talent to do it for You

Do you remember Jeff, the slick sales guy with snake skinned boots who sold high end real estate training? One of the things he promised in his presentation was that you would leave the $5000 conference with a team of professionals who had flipped multi-million dollar homes many times, and they would walk you through the entire process. He had financial experts on his team who would help you buy the homes with no money down. He had real estate agents who would find the properties for you. He had every position needed already filled, so you as the business owner didn't need to have any knowledge about real estate.

Let's think about this. If Jeff really does have a team of real estate expert employees sitting around waiting for people to come along to become millionaires, why don't they just flip the houses and become millionaires themselves? If you need no experience, no credit, and no money to do it, Jeff is really just looking for a warm body. He is looking for a warm body with $5000 to invest in the training that he knows will get you nowhere.

I hear this theory proposed at many small business conferences. It goes something like this:

"We live in a world where any skill, any resource, any knowledge that you don't currently have, is available at your fingertips through online, overseas workers. That means that even if you have never written a book, an overseas virtual writer can do it for you! If you have never balanced your checkbook, it's not a problem! If you don't know how to do sales, you don't have to learn those skills! Everything you need to run a business can be hired out for as little as $3 an hour. It has never been easier or less expensive to build a thriving business!"

It may sound motivational and inspiring, but it isn't the truth.

My good friend, Jenny, found this out for herself. Jenny has a real estate staging company. She works with high end sellers to make their vacant homes saleable. She loves working with her clients and is very good at what she does.

What she does not enjoy is everything else related to her business. She hates sales. She hates social media. She hates bookkeeping. She hates emails. She hates following up. She hates prioritizing her time. I think you get the picture.

Jenny was sitting on a bean bag up in front at a Business Intensive Retreat. We were talking about hiring out sales, and her face was glowing. "Do you mean I can just hire out all marketing and sales? That would make me so happy!"

> Weak leadership attracts weak followers.

My reply clarified. "Yes! You can and should hire everything out! That is the goal! But--you have to figure out how to make it work first. If you want to hire out your sales, you have to write your sales script first, test it to make sure it works, then train someone in your system. The system that you, as the business owner, have carefully crafted and designed."

Jenny was undaunted. "But if I can just hire a really good salesperson, they will be able to write the script for me. They would do a better job than I would ever be able to do because they are already good at that."

I didn't feel like getting into a fight. "Try it. Let me know how it works."

I don't have to tell you the results. Weak leadership attracts weak followers. She was unable to find that really good salesperson who would want to, in effect, become his or her own boss.

If your employees wanted to become business owners, they would have done that. They didn't. Instead, they are employees because they want a job. They want the security and leadership of somebody else telling them what their job is and how to do it. It feels comfortable and secure. That safety and security is what Jenny was seeking when she wanted a salesperson to create the job parameters for her. In that moment, Jenny wanted to be an employee. She wanted her employee to become the boss.

The unsexy truth is small business owners have to wear multiple hats, and they have to become fluent in all of those hats. When I hired an SEO guy to optimize my website, I don't have to become an SEO guru. What I do need to know is what I am looking for: what are the basic strategies involved, how do I track them, how do I measure results, what are the shortcuts they might try to take, and what are acceptable levels of improvement month to month. The same thing goes for any position.

If Jenny wants to hire a salesperson, she needs to be fluent in sales. She needs to know what a good sales script looks like, what the conversion ratios should be, how to overcome specific objections in her business, areas where the salesperson might overpromise to get the sale, etc.

> The process of becoming is more valuable than any yacht that the universe could deliver to you.

You can't hire talent to do it all for you. What you can do is become talented enough yourself to set up an organized, predictable system so you can then attract the talent. Hiring out is important, but it is a later step for Jenny instead of the first.

So now you know that the road to successful entrepreneurship won't be easy. It won't be fast. There is no magic pill. There is no perfect business and MLM's aren't a quick fix either. And you can't just hire it all out or throw money at it to be successful.

No, you are on the journey to *becoming*, my dear. You are about to step into getting a business education. After applying the skills and training in this book, give or take ten years, you will become a knowledgeable business owner who is capable of growing any business. You will have the financial resources, leadership skills, and know-how to take on any project that inspires you. You can run for office, do humanitarian work, invest in other businesses, you name it. You will be a force for good in this world. And the process of becoming is more valuable than any yacht that the universe could deliver to you.

Here are your action steps for this chapter:

- Cancel all motivational trainings that are on your calendar.

- Sign up for my Business Intensive Retreat or a business class at your local college instead: How to Build a Website, How to Speak in Public, or How to Master Excel. You get the idea.

CHAPTER 2

THE TRUTH ABOUT YOUR BUSINESS

Melody is an attractive, well-dressed woman with a cute brunette bob and a spunky personality. I had met her at a networking event, and she bounced up to me and started talking. In our brief conversation she mentioned that she had many opportunities in front of her as a fitness expert including a book, TV show, a radio show, and even a government appointment in Washington. She was excited about all of the prospects in her career.

While we were talking though, something triggered my honesty radar. Melody was vague about the details of these opportunities. I was curious to get to the bottom of her story when she reached out to me a few days later to schedule a phone consult.

I jumped right in on our phone call. "Tell me about the prospects you have, one by one."

She replied, "Well, I'm so excited about the TV show. I've had several people reach out to me and I could be a host, or I could even have my own show. I could do something with weight loss or nutrition, or just living out loud, you know? I could also have a radio show . . ."

I cut her off. "Tell me about the TV show. Have you been contacted by a producer?"

"Well, yeah, they want me to host a show on weight loss and I could also. . ."

I interrupted her off again. "So, who is 'they'? Have you been invited to create a pilot? Attend an audition?"

She skirted the question again. "No, I haven't auditioned or anything. But some producers in Park City want me to do a pilot for them on nutrition and how I lost weight and I could. . ."

I had to interrupt again. "Who is the producer?"

"Well, I don't know his name, but I met him at . . ."

I finally had to get out the big guns: brutal honesty.

"Melody, do you mind if I am dead honest with you?"

"Of course not," is always the hesitant reply.

"It sounds like there aren't details here--you don't have names or dates or details. Could it be that the TV show is a goal you could work towards, but there haven't been any concrete offers in reality?"

Long, stunned pause.

Melody went into defense mode. "I didn't agree to be on this call with you to be attacked. I do have prospects of a book and a TV show and a radio show. No, it might not happen this month. And it might not even happen this year, but people are reaching out to me. I have people all the time reaching out to me and wanting to work with me."

You find out a lot about people when they are backed into a corner. You find out how deep the self-deception goes. Melody is an extreme case of not being able to face where her business actually was.

After a little more dead honesty on my end the conversation turned to tears. She finally admitted the truth. "I feel like such a failure. I have been working on this business for so long, but I don't have any prospects and I haven't made any money, and I am just about to give up and get a job. I am so embarrassed."

I get excited when clients get dead honest.

I continued my conversation with Melody. "Are you kidding? I am so excited for you! Now that you are no longer pretending, you can start to make real progress! The first step of any journey is to define the starting point. When you are afraid to face that your business is at a point A, and pretend that it is at a point D, you can't move. You don't let yourself go from A to B to C and eventually get to point D because you are pretending you are already at D. Now that you know where you are, you are at a place of power for probably the first time. I am so excited for you!"

Just like Melody, many entrepreneurs struggle with admitting where they are at in business, point A. You might feel that if you have to get brutally, full-frontal honest, you would realize that even after years of saying you are in business, of working hard to spin your wheels, of pouring time and money into your business, you might still be at a point A standstill.

> I challenge you to get brutally honest with your business and not give yourself an easy grade.

To determine exactly where you are in business, we need to first take a business evaluation. Please don't skip this step or pretend your way through it. I challenge you to get brutally honest with your business and not give yourself an easy grade. Recognize that if you are at a point A in your business, that is cause for celebration! You would then know exactly where you stand and can progress from there.

Answer the following questions by selecting the answer that sounds most like your business right now, at this point of time. If your company was in a better place last year than it is right now, you will still select the answer that reflects where your company is right now.

Sometimes people get really defensive when they take this evaluation. Their comments are, "I don't have to have a big business to be successful in business! I don't need to have a team of employees, and I don't need to run my business like a corporation!" That is all true. You don't have to do anything. You can run a small business, and stay at a point A in many areas of your business for as long as you would like. If you don't feel ready to grow your business right now, I am not saying you have to.

Can I add a "but"? If you feel a lot of emotion coming up for you as you take this, and those emotions are usually defensiveness and anger, I would question if you really are happy with your business as it is.

> The reason you are at point A in business most likely has nothing to do with your talent, and definitely doesn't reflect on your worth or value as a person.

Pay attention to the emotion: maybe the anger comes from wanting to grow your business, but believing you don't have the talent? Or maybe the defensiveness comes from believing your current results in business are a reflection of your worth?

I want to assure you that the reason you are at point A in business most likely has nothing to do with your talent, and definitely doesn't reflect on your worth or value as a person. It just means that you haven't received training, or haven't implemented training. That's it. There is no judgment against you, so there is nothing to defend against. We are just looking at the state of your business.

If emotion comes up for you as you take this business evaluation, this might be a great opportunity for you to explore the common false belief that you are your business. I can assure you, you are not.

Let's jump in. For each question, choose the answer that sounds most like you.

Leadership

1. I have employees or contractors on my team and manage them effectively.

___ A. I work entirely on my own, or get some help from family and friends but no one is paid.
___ B. I hire some workers, but their hours aren't regular.
___ C. I have workers, but they often are expected to self-manage. I have basic job outlines set up, but I don't have standards for each position in place.
___ D. I have a staff of workers with regular hours and a regular schedule. I have set specific tasks for them to do, the standards of each task, and when each task should be completed. I follow up with them to ensure tasks are done on time and to standard.

2. I have regularly scheduled weekly meetings with my team.
___ A. I don't have a team.
___ B. I meet periodically with people but not on a schedule.
___ C. I have a scheduled meeting but we miss it more often than I would like.
___ D. My team meets every week, same day and the same time.

3. I have regular one-on-one sit-downs with my team members.
___ A. I don't have a team.
___ B. I don't do serious sit downs; my employees are my friends!
___ C. I sit down with people one-on-one when there is a problem or I try to address problems with the entire team.
___ D. I have regularly scheduled one-on-ones with each worker whether or not there is a problem.

4. If I have a problem with an employee who isn't doing his or her job to standards, I:
___ A. I don't have a team.
___ B. I am friends with all of my employees and we don't have problems.
___ C. I talk to them, but don't always follow up consistently.
___ D. I have an action plan set up with follow-through to remedy the situation. If employees don't improve to the level of standard, I let them go.

5. I regularly get training and have a business mentor/mastermind group.

___ A. No, I haven't given myself permission or don't believe I have the money to get training.

___ B. I go to training events but sometimes pretend that I have it all figured out.

___ C. I am sometimes learning, but I am so busy doing I don't always make the time.

___ D. I am always enrolled in a course, implementing (not just reading) strategies from a book, or working with a mentor.

Leadership Score: Record how many of each letter:

A _____
B _____
C _____
D _____

Marketing

1. I have a predictable marketing plan. I know how many leads I need to bring in to have how many sales conversations to have how many sales.

___ A. I don't have a structured marketing plan.

___ B. I work with a flash in the pan strategy--marketing pushes that are sometimes successful, but not regular or predictable.

___ C. I don't know my numbers, but I work really hard and pull in sales on a regular basis.

___ D. I know my numbers. If I needed 10 sales tomorrow, I could tell you how many leads I would need and how I could get those leads.

2. I have an online presence which includes a professional website, have a presence in all social media, use an email service provider (ESP), and have a way to collect leads online.

___ A. I spend a lot of time on social media, telling myself I am building my business.

___ B. I am working on my website, working on social media, and working to set up my ESP.

___ C. I have all of the above list set up, but everything isn't as predictable and regular as I would like.

___ D. My website looks great; I have a presence in all social media and am active in at least one; I use an email service provider and send out content at least once a month; I have an email database of clients, prospective clients, and previous clients.

3. I pay for advertising or lead generation.

___ A. I don't believe I have any money to spend on advertising/lead generation.

___ B. I would like to start with paid ads, but don't really know how to get started.

___ C. I pay for a few ads, but they aren't strategic or tracked.

___ D. I don't have enough money to NOT spend on advertising/lead generation! I know how much each lead is worth to me, and strategically select marketing venues that bring in a good ROI (return on investment).

4. My business has a predictable, reliable system for having sales conversations with prospective clients and conducts sales conversations on an everyday basis.

___ A. I rarely have sales conversations.

___ B. I am overcoming my fear of sales, and I do reach out to the leads that I collect.

___ C. My company conducts a lot of sales conversations, but we handle each one on a case-by-case basis. They are all different.

___ D. All clients go through a systematized sequence that leads them from first hearing about my business, through collecting their information, nurturing that relationship, then having the sales conversation. We use a sales script. It is predictable and it works consistently.

Marketing Score: Record how many of each letter:

A _____
B _____
C _____
D _____

Product/Service & Fulfillment

*Fulfillment means the work done to fulfill on a client contract. For example, if you are a piano teacher, fulfillment would be actually teaching the piano lessons.

1. I have a core product (or service) with one to three upsells, downsells, or cross-sells, including a high-end product or service.

___ A. I love to create product. I am currently creating something new, or improving current product, and I haven't sold much because I am still creating.

___ B. I have a core product that is complete and ready to be sold, today.

___ C. I have a core product and several other products that are complete and ready to be sold, today.

___ D. My product line-up has products in different price points. I have a high-end product and I have a predictable, systematized sequence to make sales offers.

2. I am no longer involved in the day to day production or fulfillment of the service in my business.

___ A. My company doesn't yet sell product on a regular basis or doesn't yet fulfill on a service with clients on a daily basis.

___ B. I am doing all of the product manufacturing or service fulfillment myself.

___ C. I hire out a portion of the product manufacturing or the service fulfillment.

___ D. I pass the bus test. If I were hit by a bus tomorrow, my clients would still receive my product or would still receive my services without interruption.

3. I have a freebie product (even in a service business) to give to people to sample my business, or a loss-leader product that is very inexpensive.

___ A. I have products/services here and there that I am creating but don't completely understand the relationship between them.

___ B. I have a core product/service, and have a system in place to upsell or cross sell into another product/service.

___ C. I have products/services at all levels, but limited sequences or systems to lead clients through them.

___ D. All potential clients go through my product funnel. They are invited to get my freebie, then my loss leader, then my core product/service, then upsells, downsells, or cross sells. It is predictable and systematized.

4. I have researched, determined, and taken action on the most cost efficient way to manufacture my product or fulfill on my service.
___ A. I am still trying to iron down my product/service.
___ B. I create my product with my own two hands or I fulfill on my service with my own time. I don't know exactly how much time I spend on this.
___ C. I hire out a portion of my product manufacturing or service fulfillment, and I haven't calculated my exact cost per unit or cost per fulfillment.
___ D. I can't afford NOT to hire out labor! I hire out manufacturing or hire out fulfillment of services. I have researched and use inexpensive labor if possible to save on costs. I know how much each unit costs me to manufacture, and I know how much each service costs me to fulfill.

5. My product or service is unique and different from all of my competitors' products or services.
___ A. I don't know who my competitors are.
___ B. I believe what makes my business stand apart is me. I am unique.
___ C. I focus my branding and advertising on something that is a good feature, but may not be very unique (i.e. I have great customer service).
___ D. I have researched my competition and know what sets me apart. I focus my advertising and branding on what makes my company unique. I have developed my brand around this.

Product Score: Record how many of each letter:

A _____
B _____
C _____
D _____

Customer Service

1. My clients/customers move through a predictable sequence of steps as soon as they become my client/customer.
___ A. I don't have enough clients to determine what the system would be.
___ B. Clients usually get everything they need eventually, but it is all done on a case-by-case basis.
___ C. I have some sequences that are built into a system, but others that are just left up to remembering, or on an as-needed basis.
___ D. My business has a series of checklists that ensures clients move through the correct sequence of actions at a certain pace, predictably every time.

2. I use my ESP (email service provider) with autoresponders to communicate with customers in an automated way.
___ A. I don't use an ESP.
___ B. I use an ESP that doesn't allow for multiple autoresponders.
___ C. I have a more robust ESP, but I haven't put it to use for customer service.
___ D. My business uses an ESP to automate every sequence possible for customer service.

3. I regularly ask my customers for feedback about their experience.
___ A. I don't have regular clients.
___ B. I sometimes ask clients about their experience, but it isn't systematized.
___ C. My business has a system to ask people for feedback, but it isn't always followed.
___ D. My business has a predictable, systematized way to ask clients for feedback on a regular, ongoing basis.

4. My clients/customers can easily contact my business if they are unsatisfied and receive a quick professional response.
___ A. I don't have many clients/customers who need to contact me.
___ B. My clients can contact me through my personal email or personal phone. It isn't very professional at times, and there may be a child crying in the background.

___ C. My business is easily contacted via phone, email or livechat, but customers sometimes wait longer than 24 hours to hear back from us or slip through the cracks entirely.

___ D. My business is easily contacted via phone, email or livechat. Customers are contacted within 24 hours of reaching out without exception.

5. I regularly reach out to my clients/customers to grow the relationship and offer value.

___ A. I don't have many clients/customers to build a relationship with.

___ B. I go by my gut. If I feel like I should reach out to a client, I do.

___ C. I have built out communication during the prospective client phase, but once they become clients my business doesn't have a predictable, systematized way to communicate with them.

___ D. My business has a predictable, systematized way to communicate with all current and previous clients. I employ a method that works, whether it is through email, mailers, or even a phone call schedule that my business follows.

Customer Service Score: Record how many of each letter:

A _____
B _____
C _____
D _____

Finance & Accounting

1. I use double entry accounting using financial software for business (i.e. QuickBooks).

___ A. I don't track finances and haven't completely separated my home finances from business finances (i.e. separate checking account, credit card, etc).

___ B. I track finances, possibly in a spreadsheet or Quicken (personal finance software).

___ C. I use Quickbooks, but not to its fullest extent. Rather than using accounts payable and receivable, I track income and

expenses after they happen.
___ D. I use QuickBooks & use the double entry accounting system to its fullest, using accounts payable and receivable.

2. I have built a team of financial experts.
___ A. I don't talk to anyone except my tax prep person on an annual basis.
___ B. I do bookkeeping myself and go to my CPA with any questions.
___ C. I use a bookkeeper on a regular basis.
___ D. I have a bookkeeper to record and check financial data on a weekly basis and use a CPA to advise me on financial and tax implications on a quarterly basis.

3. I run monthly reports: Profit & Loss, Cash Flow, and a Balance Sheet.
___ A. I don't know what these are.
___ B. I run a profit & loss report every month, but that is about it.
___ C. I run all of these reports, but don't always understand how to interpret the data.
___ D. I run all of these reports each month and understand how to interpret the health and growth of my company based on these reports.

4. I can look at a balance sheet and tell how financially healthy my business is.
___ A. I don't know what a balance sheet is.
___ B. I could create a balance sheet if I needed to, but I couldn't tell you what it meant about the health or growth of my company.
___ C. I am starting to understand the relationship between accounts payable, accounts receivable, equity, and cash flow.
___ D. I understand my balance in accounts payable and have that money in cash set aside. I understand my balance in accounts receivable, and when I will have those funds available. I understand how much cash I have and how much I need to run my company on a monthly basis. I understand how much equity I have in my company and how much my company is worth.

5. I manage my cash flow carefully. I have business savings and tax savings.

___ A. I don't manage my cash flow at all.

___ B. I know generally how much it takes to run my company each month. I try to keep enough money in the bank to satisfy that number.

___ C. I am starting to build up a cash reserve in savings for my business.

___ D. I know how much cash I need to run my company on a monthly basis, and am saving up for three months of operating expenses. I have tax savings as well.

Finance/Accounting Score: Record how many of each letter:

A _____
B _____
C _____
D _____

Total Business Score

You will now add up all of the A's, all of the B's, and so forth and put your final scores here:

A _____
B _____
C _____
D _____

Which letter got the highest number? This determines at which level your business is currently operating.

If your business is not where you want it to be, I plead with you not to get discouraged. There is no way to get to a level D without having gone through the other stages first. Wherever you are is the perfect place to be.

If you have been in business for a while and find yourself at a point A, you are not alone. There are many business owners who have muddled through, without getting the training they need. It is also very likely that even if you have worked with business coaches in the past, or even if you have a degree in marketing, many of the systematizing practices introduced in this evaluation are brand new to you. You can learn this quickly, and if you stick with me through the rest of this book, you will learn it now!

Here is a description of where your business is at each of these levels:

Level A: I want to have a business

If you are at a level A, you are new to business, or else new to business systems. You aren't yet working with clients on a regular, consistent basis. You are missing business fundamentals and may be operating under the belief that money is the factor that is holding you back from growing your business. Knowledge, and acting on that knowledge, is what is actually holding you back. At this stage, you may have the spirit of an entrepreneur, but you aren't yet running a business.

The example of Melody, the woman who talked about writing a book and having a TV show, is a classic example of someone who is at Level A. She has been dancing around the idea of a business for years, but she doesn't yet have a business plan or marketing plan set up. She likes to go to business networking groups to meet people and post about her industry on Facebook, but socializing does not a business make.

The first step for Melody would be to create her core product. Whether that would be a book she would write, an e-course she would provide, or a weight loss program she could launch, she would need to create an actual core product before she could begin to progress to a level B business.

If you find yourself at an A level after years of trying to launch your business, I want to emphasize that realizing you are at point A is a beautiful thing! You are now at choice: you can continue pretending that you are going to make money by doing the same things you have always done, or you can get the training you need, implement that training, and move on to a level B!

If you are brand new to business, you will of course be at a level A. Everyone has to start here. Even Bill Gates didn't get to skip levels. We all start a business at level A; having a desire to build a business, but not yet having the know-how. That is why you are reading this book. You are in the perfect place, my dear.

Level B: I am my business

Level B entrepreneurs have their basic business structure set, and are usually really good at the craftsmanship of creating the business product. Whether designing wedding gowns, training people on weight loss, or installing custom decks, you are probably a master at what you do.

Your ability to fulfill on the product or service so well may actually be holding you back from growing your business. Counterintuitive as it may seem, if you are too good at what you do, you often lose perspective of the business as a whole and focus instead on creating an impeccable product or service.

Impeccable product is impeccable product. But impeccable product does not mean you have an impeccable business. Your time as a business owner is best spent working on leading your business, not being an employee in it.

To grow to the next level, you will write out a step-by-step sequence of exactly how to create your impeccable product or service, and then you will hire people to create the impeccable product or service for you. Once all five areas of your business have been systematized through this sequence, (and those five areas are leadership, marketing/sales, finance/accounting, customer service/fulfillment, and product development) and then hired out, you will then be on your way to having not only an impeccable product, but an impeccable business!

Level C: Some systems are in place

Level C business owners know their role in their business. You are no longer stuck in the I-must-do-it-all-myself mentality. You are starting to systematize and hire out pieces of the business, but may get bogged down in solving day-to-day fires that seem to arise constantly.

The secret to pulling out of the day-to-day firefighter role is to dig deep for a little while. Yes, you will have to put in extra hours to work on the business, systematizing a sequence for every fire that you put out, in addition to actually putting out the fires at the same time. There is no shortcut here--you can continue to tell yourself you are putting in your max and get frustrated with the obvious holes in your system, or you can put on your big girl shoes, and work your tail off for the next year until you completely systematize your business. It will be hard. And it will be worth it.

Level D: You work ON your business and not IN your business

Congratulations! You understand that the real product you have is not the product or service your company sells; rather, the business is the product. You have set up your business to run smoothly and systematically with or without you. You are now in prime position to sell your business if desired and move on to your next venture. For your next venture, I challenge you to start or purchase a business that is bigger than your first. Stretch yourself!

If you want to hold on to your business at this point, continue to systematize, automate and hire yourself out of the business almost entirely. Get your weekly maintenance work hours down to only a few hours per week. You will then be free to (a) grow your business in new ways, (b) start another business, or (c) sell your business or (d) use your expertise and resources and start a non-business venture.

At Level D business owner, you are a powerful creator. Offers to work with others on exciting projects will be falling into your lap, and the challenge for you will be to turn down the many opportunities that may be good, but aren't exactly what you want for your life. Sometimes having amazing opportunities is a more difficult challenge than having no opportunities!

Here are your action steps for this chapter:

- Take the Business Level Questionnaire honestly

- Score your results

CHAPTER 3

THE TRUTH ABOUT WHAT YOU REALLY WANT

"He who has a Why to live for can bear almost any How."
-Nietzsche

What do you REALLY want out of your business? Think about that for a minute. Do you want prestige, money, influence, world peace? What do you really want?

In this next section, we are going to dive deep into your brain and your heart and pull out what is actually motivating you to run the business the way you are running it, and what motivated you to go into business in the first place. Once you know the core of what is motivating you, you will be able to dig deep and push through the huge challenges that you already know you are going to meet on your journey. You didn't think you were going to become a level D business owner without challenges, did you? You need to prepare your inner self with as many tools as you can to survive the marathon ahead.

In this section, I am going to ask you to access an unfiltered, unedited, unconstrained piece of you that you may not have accessed in a long time. I am also going to ask you to admit to yourself why you are running your business the way you have been running it. And if you are a "good girl" reading this, no doubt the thought of you being unfiltered and unconstrained hits a panic button for you. "What if I let all my unfiltered and unedited thoughts come to the surface? What if at my core I am truly evil? Or even worse--truly lazy? What if I go exploring in those depths and find that I have a hidden murderess inside of me? Or maybe a hidden couch potato who wants to quit her business and do nothing but watch Oprah and eat doughnuts on the couch? What if? What if? What if?"

Take a deep breath, babe. I can assure you that if you aren't an Oprah-watching-doughnut-eating-murderess now, you won't be after this exercise either. There is nothing in the depths of your soul that you don't already know is there. We are just going to go through an exercise of bringing to light what you already know. We are going to get honest about why you run your business they way that you do, and what you really want out of your business.

> If you aren't an Oprah-watching-donut-eating-murderess now, you won't be after this exercise either.

I can take a guess and say that up to this point you have probably not been honest with yourself.

You may be able to tell yourself and everyone around you, including your mom, your husband, and your church minister, pretty little lies about what you really want out of life. But those quiet inklings in your heart, that drive inside of you that pulls you on, those crazy ideas in your head that you keep trying to push down, that is what we are going to listen to today. You can let yourself think as big as you want to think; do not have your feet planted in reality during this exercise.

I am going to lead you through a journaling meditation in which you will write what your thoughts are--unedited. If they involve watching Oprah and eating doughnuts, that is exactly what you will write down. If your thoughts involve becoming a murderess, you will write that down and then call a psychiatrist and get help. Deal?

I invite you to write in this book. Up to this point, these pages might still be virgin white without a single pen mark. It's time to break the rules--write in this book! As you begin writing, there may be thoughts that come to you that would be embarrassing to write down. You may not want to admit that you hate your current business. You may not want to admit that you actually have very big, very bold dreams. I dare you to write down the truth anyway.

Read this next section one paragraph at a time. Stop after reading each paragraph and do what it instructs you to do. No funny stuff here, just getting to the bottom of what your business motivation is.

This section will be completely devoid of power if you just read through the exercises. However, if you take your time to think through each exercise, getting still and quiet before each one, this will be one of the most powerful experiences you have had in a long time. I dare you to play full out on this one.

Let's take a minute to explore the current realities of your business, with the goal of understanding why things are the way they are so we can then change them. We just went through the quiz of what you are doing, now we are going to explore why you are doing them.

Take a minute to feel grounded and peaceful. Close your eyes. Take three deep breaths. Now go through the following exercise, answering the why questions.

Leadership

1. If you don't have employees or are understaffed, why have you not invested? If your belief is you can't afford employees, have you considered your time as free? If so, how is the belief that your time is worthless affecting your business?

_____
_____
_____
_____
_____

2. If you aren't regularly meeting with your team as a group and on an individual basis, why haven't you? Are you treating your employees like objects that you don't need to deal with unless necessary? Do you feel inadequate as a leader and are avoiding meeting with them? Are you afraid of showing up like the boss?

_____
_____
_____
_____
_____

3. If you aren't having those hard conversations with your employees, telling them directly what is not working for you on a regular basis, why aren't you? Are you afraid they won't like you? Are you afraid you will hurt their feelings? Are you afraid they will quit? Are you afraid of losing control in the conversation and appearing weak? Are you treating them as if they are fragile and will break? Why haven't you had the hard conversations that you have needed to have?

_____
_____
_____
_____
_____

4. If you aren't working with coaches or mentors and regularly getting training in business, why aren't you? Do you feel you should be able to figure it out on your own? Do you have a hard time trusting others? Are you too ashamed to admit to a mentor what the current state of your business is? Are you afraid to look as if you don't have it all figured out?

_____
_____
_____
_____
_____

Marketing

1. If you don't have a well-defined marketing plan, why don't you? Do you need training in this area and haven't reached out for it? Why haven't you reached out for training? Have you been afraid to risk money on training? Do you avoid making plans because you fear being controlled? Is the chaos and drama of running without a plan a thrill for you?

_____
_____
_____
_____
_____

2. If you don't have a complete and professional online presence, why don't you? Are you afraid of technology? Do you tell yourself (i.e. lie to yourself) that you like being old school? Do you need training in this area and haven't reached out for it? Why haven't you? Do you feel that you are too old to learn technology? Do you feel that you have to master everything yourself? Have you not paid for professional services because you don't value your business/yourself enough to spend money on it?

_____
_____
_____
_____
_____

3. If you aren't spending money to get leads or to advertise, why aren't you? Is your marketing plan not consistent enough in following up with the leads you already have? Why is that? Do you need training in this area and haven't reached out for it?

_____
_____
_____
_____
_____

4. If you are avoiding the sales conversation, or are not charging enough for your products/services, why is that? Are you afraid to ask people for money? Do you feel that your service is something that should be available to everyone, regardless of their ability (or desire) to pay? Do you doubt that your product, service, or even you is worth money? Are you afraid that people will think you are greedy or money-centered? Are you in the habit of always discounting your product? Why?

_____
_____
_____
_____
_____

Product/Service Fulfillment

The word "product" refers to either a physical product or a service

1. If you don't have a core product to sell yet, or are constantly changing your core product, why is that? Are you afraid to move from the production stage of business into the marketing and sales stage? Have you not made it a priority? Why not? Are you afraid to ask people for money? Do you believe your product has no value unless it is perfect?

_____
_____
_____
_____
_____

2. If you manufacture a product, why are you still doing that with your own two hands? If you have a service business, why are you still personally fulfilling on the service? Are you afraid of what growing a business would mean for you personally? For your family? Are you afraid of your potential? Do you believe that no one could create the product as well as you, or fulfill on the service as well as you? Do you believe that you ARE the business? Do you think everything would fall apart if you didn't have a hand in it? Do you believe that clients really do just want you and would be unwilling to pay if the service was fulfilled by anyone else? Do you tell yourself you really just enjoy that part of the business, even when sometimes that isn't true? Are you missing the bigger picture of business; that your time and energy is better spent in leadership and working on the business, not as an employee in it? Do you believe that your worth comes from fulfilling in your business?

_____
_____
_____
_____

_____

_____

3. If you don't have a consistent product funnel that people move through in a systematic manner, why don't you? If you have product ideas but haven't created them yet, why is that? Do you need training in this area and haven't reached out for it? Are you stuck on perfecting one product? Why is that?

_____

_____

_____

_____

_____

4. If you haven't researched the most inexpensive ways to manufacture your products, why haven't you? If you aren't using the least expensive labor force, why aren't you? Are you afraid of trusting people you don't personally know? Are you afraid to trust people who come from different cultures or countries than you? Why are you afraid to trust? Do you consistently pay people more than the job is worth so you don't hurt their feelings?

_____

_____

_____

_____

_____

5. If your product/service isn't truly unique, why haven't you made it unique? Do you believe that being you is enough to make your product unique? Are you afraid to step out of the box and do something truly unique because it will make you stand out? Are you afraid of being noticed? Are you guilty of telling yourself that your product is unique when in reality it blends into the sea of other products just like yours? Is there a false sense of pride (i.e. insecurity) there that is preventing you from making changes to your product?

_____

_____

_____

_____

_____

_____

Customer Service

1. If your client flow doesn't move through a series of predictable, sequenced steps, why doesn't it? Do you tell yourself that each client is different, therefore deserves a completely different experience? Is that really true? Why are you holding on to that? Do you need training in this area and haven't reached out for it? Have you not thought through and planned out what your client flow is? Why haven't you?

_____

_____

_____

_____

_____

2. If your customer communication isn't automated as much as it possibly could be, why isn't it? Are you afraid of technology? Do you need training in this area and haven't reached out for it? Are you afraid to send an automated email instead of a personal phone call because you don't want to hurt anyone's feelings? If so, why are you afraid of people?

_____

_____

_____

_____

_____

3. If you aren't asking every client for feedback in a predictable, systematized way, why aren't you? Are you afraid of getting negative feedback? Are you only asking customers who are raving fans for feedback? Are you discounting customers' opinions who have had a negative experience? Do you tell yourself that any upset customers are just crazy and impossible to please? If so, why?

_____

_____

_____

_____

_____

4. If your clients can't contact your business easily and expect a prompt, professional response, why haven't you made this a requirement? Are you running your business so chaotically that you don't value your existing clients? Do you need to hire someone to manage your customer service? Why haven't you done that?

_____

_____

_____

_____

_____

5. If you aren't continuing to build and nurture the relationship you have with existing clients, why aren't you doing that? Have you been in the habit of treating existing clients like dollar signs--only reaching out to get the initial sale? Have you neglected to provide upsells for existing clients? Why?

_____

_____

_____

_____

_____

Finance

1. If you don't have QuickBooks (or other similar software) and aren't using it to its fullest potential, why aren't you? Do you need training for this software and haven't reached out for it? Why haven't you? Are you telling yourself that your spreadsheet system is adequate? If so, why are you defending mediocrity? Are you telling yourself that you can't afford it? Why?

_____

_____

_____

_____

_____

2. If you don't have a finance team including a regular bookkeeper and a CPA to consult with, why don't you? Are you pretending that if you don't think about finances they will go away? Do you expect yourself to wear every hat in your business and be good at everything? Are you too embarrassed to reach out for help because you know so little about finances or because your books are such a mess?

_____
_____
_____
_____
_____

3. If you aren't looking at finance reports on a monthly basis, why aren't you? Are you needing basic business finance training and haven't reached out for it? Are you trying to avoid the reality that the numbers are showing? Are you avoiding things that are not fun? Why?

_____
_____
_____
_____
_____

4. If you are having a problem with cash flow, why is that? Are you needing basic business finance training and haven't reached out for it? Are you being too aggressive in growing your business? If so, why are you so impatient to grow? Do you need to take loans out but haven't? Are you trying to bootstrap a business that really needs funding? Why?

_____
_____
_____
_____
_____
_____

That exercise can be a little heavy when you work through it, but I am hoping you had some meaningful insights. Here are some insights that previous high-level clients of mine have had. Keep in mind that these comments come from people with established businesses, who are what you would describe as business rockstars. We all have insecurities that hold us back!

- I haven't hired out certain positions because I am a control freak. I like to have everything just the way I want it. I expect perfection out of myself.

- I forget to do private meetings with my employees because I don't want to give negative feedback. I don't want to make them feel bad. I think I have to protect my employees from having bad feelings.

- I haven't reached out to a coach because I am afraid to let someone see what my business is really like. I am also afraid that anyone knowing my business will steal my business idea. I'm also afraid that if I work with a coach I will be asked to go to the next level and I am afraid I'm not ready. I am afraid I'm not good enough and my product isn't good enough yet.

- I have discounted my products because I have been in the mindset that it is hard to get people to invest. I just got into the habit of discounting, and haven't ever stopped.

- I haven't upgraded my website because I don't know how to do it myself and don't feel in control when working with people who know the technology better than I do. I have been scared of learning new things.

- I have another product I want to add to my business, but I have been too scared of overwhelming my employees. I have put their imagined feelings ahead of the success of my business.

- I have been telling myself that there is no way to predict what my clients need because they are all different, but that isn't true. I have just been putting off planning it. I haven't been delivering the high quality service I could be.

- I don't ask for feedback from my customers because I am afraid I let people down a lot. I am afraid they are just pretending that they like my product. I am afraid that my customers haven't received any benefit, and that I am a failure.

The first step to making a change is just to see the problem. Celebrate! You have just seen the problem: you. And that is a powerful truth to realize, not because we are condemning or shaming ourselves, but because we now know we have the power to change anything we want to!

> The first step to making a change is just to see the problem. Celebrate! You have just seen the problem: you.

Even if you are lacking know-how, it is you who has chosen not to reach out and get training. It is you who has shrunk from fears and chosen to play small. That is the good news! The ball is in your court; you are in full control here. You can change your business.

Now that we have explored where you are in your business and why you are there, let's take an honest look at where you want to be.

This is the fun part! How does your business now compare with its true potential and your real dreams?

Here are your action steps for this chapter:

- Answer all five "hat" questions honestly. Take your time and go through them slowly.

CHAPTER 4

THE BIG VISION

I am going to take you through another writing exercise that will access those repressed parts of you that are screaming to come out. Remember: don't edit yourself, and dismiss any "I could never do that!" thoughts.

EXERCISE 1: Take a minute to feel grounded and peaceful. Close your eyes. Take three deep breaths. I want you to imagine that your business has unlimited access to any resource, training, or connection you would need. There is nothing to limit your dreams or ambition--you can have anything you want.

EXERCISE 2: Now that you are peaceful and relaxed, close your eyes again and take about five minutes to imagine what the business of your dreams looks like in this unlimited space. If any thoughts of "I couldn't possibly do that" come up, and they will, gently dismiss your inner editor and allow those thoughts to come freely. If money, time, or knowledge was not an obstacle, and you knew you couldn't fail, what would your business look like? Imagine in full-blown technicolor what the business of your dreams looks like.

EXERCISE 3: Now close your eyes again and take about five minutes and imagine what you will be doing as the president of your company on a regular, day-to-day basis. Imagine it in as much detail as possible. What would you be doing today as the president of the business of your dreams?

EXERCISE 4: Now close your eyes again and take about five minutes to imagine what you will be doing on your highlight reel. Every business has great highlights, whether they happen once a month, once a quarter, or several times a year. Imagine what those business highlights will be and imagine them in as much detail as possible.

EXERCISE 5: Now close your eyes again and go back to the thoughts of your business as it is today. What is the first thing you need to do, learn, or implement to move in the direction of your big dream?

Whew! I love taking people through the Big Vision exercise. If you had a difficult time imagining anything bigger than your business making 10% more income and maybe, just maybe, having a few employees, I invite you to revisit this exercise again in a few months. Watch as your vision gradually expands, and you are able to start thinking bigger.

The goal of this big-vision activity is to start looking for patterns in your big vision, not pinpoint exactly how your life with play out.

If your vision is so big that it may as well be a Hollywood movie, congratulate yourself for having big vision! Please know that just because you had this particular vision on this day in this year, it doesn't mean this particular vision will come to be. As you probably remember from chapter 1, I don't believe in any magic secrets. Today you had this vision for your life, tomorrow you may have another.

The goal of this Big Vision activity is to start looking for patterns in your big vision, not to pinpoint exactly how your life will play out.

While this meditation exercise is still fresh in your head, answer the following questions:

1. What does your business look like?

2. What do you do as president of the business on a daily basis? What are you during those highlights?

3. What is the first thing you need to do, learn, or implement to move in the direction of your big dream?

Here are your action steps for this chapter:

- Do all five Big Vision exercises

- Write out the three Big Vision questions

CHAPTER 5

THE TRUTH ABOUT ARRIVING

In the last section, you hopefully imagined a big, beautiful business (and life) in full technicolor. Maybe you spoke to thousands from a stage. Maybe you wore designer shoes that clicked as you walked down the marble floor of your office. Maybe your business had a huge charity program.

Whatever those dreams are, in our beginning stage of business we tend to think, "I will have made it when I am (fill in your big goals here). I will feel so accomplished and so fulfilled when I reach that point." Unfortunately, that is not how it will play out.

Before you start imagining all of the happiness that the business of your dreams would bring to your life, I have to wax philosophical.

As you start to have success in your business, you will realize that the joy doesn't come from reaching those pinnacles or peaks. The platitude is true: the joy comes from the journey.

I met a woman in an unexpected place who lived this principle. I was at a popular ice cream parlor while ago, and as usual there was a long line that moved very slowly down the middle of the store. I am not known for my patience, and by the time I made my way up to the ice cream counter I was not in the mood to be happy or to feel fulfilled. I just wanted my five dollar ice cream cone.

That is when I met the young woman scooping ice cream.

She looked directly at me and held my gaze for a few seconds. Despite the line, and my impatient attitude, she was really seeing me. She offered me an ice cream sample, and told me what her favorite flavor was. She was friendly in an easy way—nothing felt forced. After I made my selection, she told me my ice cream choice was elegant. She patiently waited while I counted out change. I felt her presence.

> I want to propose to you that your business has as much power to bring you fulfillment right now as it does when you reach any of those pinnacles you imagine in your dreams.

Strange as it sounds, a woman who scooped ice cream for me months ago had a prevalent, lasting effect on how I approach life and business. She has inspired me to be more present in my own work. There is no arriving; I have to catch myself when I find myself striving for success and not enjoying every moment in my business.

What if your business has the capacity right now of giving you the kind of fulfillment and joy you are looking for in your dreams? What if you living your life in a present way, really seeing each client you work with, can change lives in and of itself? If a woman scooping ice cream can emit joy and fulfillment, what if you could do the same thing? What if you felt fulfillment when downloading reports from QuickBooks, giving your employee feedback, designing a Facebook Ad, or writing an autoresponder?

I want to propose to you that your business has as much power to bring you fulfillment right now as it does when you reach any of those pinnacles you imagine in your dreams.

I told a client of mine this yesterday.

Elaine is a younger version of me. She also wears a short, red bob. Like me, she used to be a school teacher. She even has a tutoring business (how I got my start). She wants to eventually sell her business and be a speaker/trainer.

It is uncanny how much we have in common on the outside.

On the inside, we also have a lot in common. Elaine asked me in a private session, "How much time do I have until I am where you are at?" She didn't like the stage in business that she was in and wanted to fast forward five years.

I also used to dream of the day when I would achieve my goals. Thoughts ran through my head about my future. "When I make a lot of money in my business I will be successful. People will treat me differently. I will be sure of myself and confident and be a powerful businesswoman. I will feel fulfilled and happy."

In all of my mental scenarios, there would be a point in time when I would have arrived, and at that point I would then feel fulfilled and complete.

> In all of my mental scenarios, there would be a point in time when I would have arrived, and at that point I would then feel fulfilled and complete.

That was not how it played out.

Fast forward ten years. I made more money in one month than many people make in a year. My business was well on its way to being automated, and I had a fantastic team running the business. I had figured out marketing and sales, and the business ran smoothly.

One of my employees asked me, "How does it feel to make that amount of money? How does it feel to have made it?" I am sure he expected me to start jumping on the couch with joy and proclaim that I had arrived, and now felt fulfilled and complete.

He got the opposite answer. "It isn't exciting like I used to expect it would to be. I kinda miss the days when it was the great unknown. I miss the huge learning curve. I miss feeling like I am being stretched every day, and I miss feeling like I have to exercise absolute faith every day. I miss stepping into the dark."

Once you have "arrived" it is no longer the great unknown, calling to you. I am not saying reaching your goals is a disappointment by any means, but just like kids at Christmas time, most of the fun comes from the anticipation of the day. You will probably look back one day, having "arrived" and appreciate the journey much more than you do now.

I believe the purpose of being here on earth is to grow and learn. There is no point in our lives when we will have learned it all, no point when we will decide that no more growth is needed. A good friend of mine works with seniors in their 80's and 90's. Even at the end of their lifetime, they yearn for continued growth and learning.

I told Elaine, my red-head-bobbed client who wanted to fast forward her business five years the same thing. I told her this grueling time she is experiencing right now may even be the highlight of her entire business. She didn't believe me, and you probably don't believe me, but if you implement the strategies in this book there is a good chance you will know for yourself in a few years.

CHAPTER 6

THE TRUTH ABOUT STARTING

I hope you are on the same page with me on these two principles: (1) achieving your goals won't suddenly make your life feel worthwhile and whole if you don't already feel worthwhile and whole, and (2) most of the joy in your business will come from the growth that comes from the struggle.

Now we are going to move beyond the theory of what to expect and not expect from reaching your goals, and start talking about the how. How exactly do you move forward to achieving those big business dreams?

After going through the Big Vision exercise, you know what your big dream looks like. Now you need to ask yourself if you are willing to do what it takes to get there.

> Most things worth having in this life can't be done in one push, no matter how amazing or noble that push is.

At my Business Intensive Retreats, the clients who are ready to go to the next level in their businesses are invited to join my teamELITE, a high-end, year-long training program. I tell these women (and a few brave men) that the journey in front of them isn't going to be like one giant hill that they can will themselves up. You don't need an intense push of motivation. Most things worth having in this life can't be done in one push, no matter how amazing or noble that push is.

The hard part, and the part that most people aren't willing to do, is the every day. Doing small, seemingly insignificant things every day, one at a time, over and over again, now that is hard. You win the race by doing those unsexy, sometimes boring tasks, day after day after day. Are you willing to do that? That is much harder than one big push.

Here is your first challenge. I am asking you to go get paper and a pen.

Did you do it? Please recognize you are at choice right now. Many people will not want to do the unsexy, tedious task of getting up to get some paper. How you read this book is how you run your business. Are you willing to play full out in this exercise, even though it isn't anything super challenging? Even if it isn't noble or motivational? If you are, and are willing to do other small, seemingly insignificant tasks again and again and again, you will see success. You can reach those dreams.

Read through your Big Vision exercise answers and make a list on the paper you just got. (I am going to assume you did get off the couch; nice job). You are going to write a list of the physical, tangible pieces included in your big vision.

A common struggle for big-picture thinkers is to move that vision down from the idea or concept stage into concrete, tangible details. The phrase "heal the world" would not be concrete or tangible. Ask yourself, "What would that look like?" until you get concrete, tangible details. Again, don't edit your answers as they get more specific. Write down a bulleted list of what those tangible details would look like.

Here are some examples:

- Work with teenagers and their parents in a one-on-one setting
- Build an orphanage in Uganda
- Wear Jimmy Choo shoes

- Host an event in LA with 200 people

Go ahead and look through your Big Vision questions, filling in the details. Write down the what, where, how many, and when details.

After you have gone through your Big Vision and written out your list of concrete and tangible phrases, skim through your new list and put a star by the three or four ideas that are extra juicy for you. If you could get only a few things on that list, what would those things be? Which items make you excited just thinking about them? Don't choose the things you feel you should be excited about, and don't judge yourself for choosing the goals that most speak to you instead of the goals you feel you "should" want to work toward.

Now comes the fun part! We are going to move from the dream in the sky stage into the action stage. We are going to implement those day after day, unsexy, seemingly insignificant tasks that will take you from where you are now to where you want to be.

> The way we eat an elephant is one bite at a time. The way we reach a big goal is one small step at a time.

Choose your top dream from your starred three or four. We are going to focus on how to achieve one juicy goal. I'll choose the goal "Wear Jimmy Choo shoes" as an easy example.

The way we eat an elephant is one bite at a time. The way we reach a big goal is one small step at a time.

We are going to make a list of the micro steps you will need to do to get you moving in the direction of your goal. If you are here, at this exact point in time, with the resources and knowledge you currently have, what is the very first step to become a Jimmy Choo shoe wearing woman?

I have two rules here. The steps need to (1) take one hour or less to complete, and (2) be able to be checked off a list.

If my first microstep is, "Start wearing Jimmy Choo shoes" it does not pass the test. I wouldn't be able to buy $650 shoes in one hour. I also can't check off "start doing" off of a list. I need specific, one-hour or less action items.

This is what my micro-step list would look like:

- Search on Pinterest for Jimmy Choo shoes I like: 1 hour
- Decide on my top 3 choices
- Call stores in my area to see if they carry that shoe
- Schedule shopping trip with my daughter
- Go to store & purchase shoes
- Wear them to the event next Tuesday

There you have it; six steps to becoming a Jimmy Choo wearing woman. Maybe it would be more steps in another scenario:

- Search on Pinterest for Jimmy Choo shoes I like: 1 hour
- Decide on my top 3 choices
- Call stores in my area to see if they carry that shoe
- Schedule shopping trip with my daughter
- Go to store & try on shoes
- Set up budget to create savings each month to purchase the shoes ($100 per month for 3 months set aside)
- List my Grandmother's antique quilt for $150 on ebay
- Refer my neighbor Amy Lou to Kim Flynn Consulting and get an affiliate commission for $200
- Purchase shoes online.

Notice that money or the lack of it isn't an insurmountable obstacle. Having to budget and earn money for your dreams just adds a few more steps. Most people think having money first is a requirement to most goals. "I must be making seven figures before I would become a woman who wears Jimmy Choo shoes." Nope.

Becoming a woman who wears Jimmy Choo shoes just requires that you (a) know what your goals are, and (b) are willing to do the unsexy, day-to-day tasks (like setting up and sticking to a budget) to reach your goals. It isn't a giant mountain, just small daily tasks.

The first time you wear those Jimmy Choo's, chances are your friends will say, "Oh! Those are so cute! I could never afford those!" And you would then know the truth--yep, they could. In almost all cases, they are just choosing not to. They aren't doing the unsexy things to wear the sexy shoes.

Let's move to a more significant goal. You want to build an orphanage in Uganda. Let's say you have never been to Uganda, you don't have any experience building orphanages, and you don't have a significant amount of money in the bank.

What do you do? Here are some sample micro steps:

- Step 1: Google "How to open an orphanage in Africa". Research for one hour.
- Step 2: Call Amy Schmaby, the woman you met who does charity building projects in South America. Take her out to lunch to pick her brain.
- Step 3: Post on Facebook: "I am interested in any contacts to Uganda. Does anyone know anyone who lives there or who has lived there?"
- Step 4: Google "Orphanages near (my city)" and find the closest orphanage to my city
- Step 5: Call the orphanage and ask if they allow visitors or volunteers

There is no right answer here. If I asked 500 women what the first five micro-steps they would take to get to an orphanage in Uganda, I would get 500 different answers. It isn't about what is correct; it is about moving forward.

Now it's your turn. You will write out five micro steps for the juicy goal that you selected. What steps can you take with the connections, knowledge, and resources that you currently have to get you closer to your goal? Remember, they must (1) take one hour or less to complete, and (2) can be checked off a list.

Choose your top goal (with clarifying details added) from the Big Vision exercise.

My top goal:

_____

Step 1:

_____

_____

Step 2:

_____

_____

Step 3:

_____

_____

Step 4:

_____

_____

Step 5:

_____

_____

Before we move on from micro steps and do any more planning, go ahead and put these five items on your current to-do list, whatever that looks like for you. If you are a client of mine and have attended a Business Intensive Retreat, record this in your Plug & Play Business System with a due date.

And yes, this is another test for you. Are you willing to do this seemingly monotonous task of putting these steps on your to-do list right now? Or are you waiting for some sexier, big push task to get started? If so, you will never reach your dreams. Harsh I know, but true.

After figuring out what your first five micro steps are, we are going to move into planning out bigger MACRO steps. We obviously can't plan our business all the way from here to Uganda in micro steps today; there is too much we don't know.

What we can plan out is our anticipated MACRO steps. What big steps would you logically take to move from where you are now to where you want to be? These may be goals that take one month, one quarter, or even one year to complete. They encompass many micro steps to achieve.

> Are you willing to do this seemingly monotonous task of putting these steps on your to-do list right now? Or are you waiting for some sexier, big push task to get started? If so, you will never reach your dreams.

Let's go back to our Uganda orphanage example. Assume we have finished our first five micro steps and we have done some research about orphanages and Uganda, and have a connection to an orphanage in Mexico. What would be our next bigger MACRO step? Just like micro steps, your MACRO steps might look very different from mine. This is what I came up with:

MACRO Step 1: Volunteer in orphanage for one week to determine building, materials, and staffing requirements

MACRO Step 2: Create a plan to get funding for building materials and staffing & begin executing

MACRO Step 3: Visit Uganda and determine where there is need for an orphanage

MACRO Step 4: Assemble a 5-person volunteer group with construction experience

MACRO Step 5: Plan a trip with a volunteer group to build an orphanage

After starting this project you may realize that your MACRO's have been way off. You may realize that Uganda doesn't need orphanages, and that Haiti is where your help is more needed. You will probably change almost everything in the process, but your initial MACRO's serve to get you started.

You will set a monthly or quarterly time frame goal for each MACRO step. Because of the scope of the project in this example, I would set a quarterly goal for the first MACRO. Three months from now, we want to have completed our first MACRO step. I would plan to visit the closest orphanage and volunteer there for one week in the next three months. Then I would set up micros to complete the MACRO.

Here are some micro steps to complete the first MACRO of volunteering in an orphanage for one week.

- Step 1: Call orphanage to set volunteer date
- Step 2: Record date in my calendar
- Step 3: Plan trip itinerary: when to leave, hotel stays
- Step 4: Create list of all questions I want answered while there
- Step 5: Pack for trip

Isn't it amazing how quickly we just went from having the dream of "Someday I want to build an orphanage in Uganda" to planning a trip and making significant progress towards this goal? Setting dates and planning (and then doing) your micro steps every week to move you towards those goals is the secret.

If your eyes are glazing over at this point, now that we have moved from self-introspection to an action plan, you aren't alone. Goal setting and creating action plans isn't riveting reading. But it is what grows a business. If you want to learn how to get those big dreams of yours, keep pressing on!

Let's move back to your number one juicy goal. What are the MACRO steps you will need to accomplish after you complete your initial set of micros? Keep in mind the same rules are in place here: these must be tangible tasks that you can check off a list.

These steps will work toward the same top goal you worked on previously.

My Top Goal:

_____   _____

MACRO 1:

_____

_____

MACRO 2:

_____

_____

MACRO 3:

_____

_____

MACRO 4:

_____

_____

MACRO 5:

_____

_____

Set a goal date to complete your first MACRO. What is that date?

_____

It is amazing what will happen in your life when you begin living on purpose. You can create significant progress in a short amount of time. You know what your goals are, you know what the basic MACRO outline is to get to those big goals, and you know that all it takes to achieve those MACRO steps is to just take one small step after another. There is no magic to playing BIG, but it does require small amounts of action on a regular, consistent basis. Small, consistent action is your ticket to the universe.

I can't wait to see what you are about to create.

Here are your action steps for this chapter:

- Choose your first goal

- Write out your first five action steps

- Write out your Macros

CHAPTER 7

PLAYING BIG IN SYSTEMS

"No wise pilot, no matter how great his talent and experience, fails to use his checklist." -Charlie Munger

So far we have dispelled the myths of business, presented some unsexy realities, evaluated where you are in business right now, why you are there, and where you want to be. You are also now familiar with the micro/MACRO mindset to achieve one goal at a time.

I now have some bad news for you. The second half of this book will be even less sexy than the first part. I can't promise to keep you entertained, inspired, or even awake. What I can promise you is that you need this information. Take some caffeine pills, drink a Red Bull; do whatever you need to do, but get through this second half of the book. Engage in the material, implement the teaching, follow the steps as outlined, and your business will move to the next level.

This material is what I specialize in: content-heavy, dense training. I frequently tell my clients that this is the

> This is the "eat your broccoli" part of the training. It may not be soul-stirring, but it is nutrient-dense and essential for a healthy business.

"eat your broccoli" part of the training. It may not be soul-stirring, but it is nutrient-dense and essential for a healthy business.

The first thing we are going to do in the sections that follow is break your business into the different hats you wear as you run your business: leadership, marketing, finance, product development and customer service/fulfillment. We are going to dive into the nitty gritty. We are going to talk about what you do on a regular basis in each of these areas of your business, what systems need to be put in place, and the why and how to beat the temptations you will face in each area that, if you give into them, will keep you playing small.

After we go through systematizing all five hats, and get your business running smoothly, we will delve into how to grow your business through marketing and sales.

As I write this, I am anxious to give you everything that I know and insert it into your brain. I want to be at your side and go on this journey into the wild with you. I can't do that in a written format. A book is simply a map of the terrain. You will still have to motivate yourself to go on the hike in the first place, and you will inevitably experience tripping over rocks, taking wrong turns, and getting lost. If you are interested in hiring a guide to go with you on the hike to shortcut the process, keep you accountable, and prevent many wrong turns, I invite you to look into my coaching and training programs. I will be mentioning my Business Intensive Retreat throughout this book, and I want to encourage you to start thinking about getting yourself to one!

Why do you want to play BIG in your systems?

Becoming a successful business owner is about a lot more than creating a good product.

Let me illustrate why having your business systematized is imperative. One of the most talented graphic designers I know lives in my area. Her name is Bridget, and she has super hip spiky red hair, and dresses in seventeen layers of different patterns and fabrics and jewelry. She has a natural eye for aesthetics, and is so talented she sometimes doesn't realize that design doesn't come easily for most people. Design flows out of her as effortlessly as breathing.

After meeting her and seeing her portfolio I was extremely impressed. I negotiated with her to give my year-long teamELITE clients a package deal if I referred them to her exclusively. We worked out a package we were both happy with, and I was looking forward to seeing the new logos and website designs that she would create for my clients.

Two months later, I was no longer looking forward to seeing anything from Bridget. I could not get Bridget to respond after leaving numerous emails and phone messages over three weeks. When Bridget finally did respond, she asked for double the price we had already negotiated. I had to send her the original agreement on her own letterhead, stating the original price. I didn't hear back for weeks. When I finally did hear back, I got a quick email saying she was swamped, but she still wanted to work with my clients. Uh, no thank you.

> Your PRODUCT is not your business. Your BUSINESS is your product.

Bridget fell prey to many systematization mistakes. She believed that her product (her graphic design) was her business, in reality it is the other way around. Her BUSINESS is her product. The entire experience the client goes through is the business: seeing the marketing materials, the sales process, interaction with the employees and the experience through the fulfillment process, and how much profit the business makes on the transaction. All of these pieces work together to make up the business. The product is just one small piece. Said simply:

Your PRODUCT is not your business.
Your BUSINESS is your product.

Bridget's business was failing. I don't know if it was failing financially; she might be able to survive financially by constantly attracting unsuspecting prey, but her business is failing as a product. It is failing to provide a good service; a reliable, systematized process to lead customers successfully from first interaction through fulfillment.

And it is such a tragedy! I would recommend to Bridget (if I could ever get in touch with her) that if she doesn't want to go through the work of creating a systematized business, that she work for another company as an employee. Then she can be used in her strength--as a designer.

If your business has similarities to Bridget's, don't despair. It will take work, but I am about to show you how to build that system, a business that is whole and complete and is in its entirety, a good product.

Here are your action steps for this chapter:

- Keep reading this book

CHAPTER 8

PLAYING BIG IN LEADERSHIP

The first hat in business we are going to delve into is Leadership.

I don't believe great leaders are born. I believe great leaders follow great systems.

One of the best ways to show you what playing BIG in your leadership system looks like is to give you case studies of how one of my clients went from playing small to playing BIG in leadership in only a few months.

Melanie has a catering business. She is a mom of four, and the catering business was her husband's dream that she found herself sucked into managing. She didn't feel the call of entrepreneurship, and didn't love working with people although that is what she did every day. She was famous with the Kim Flynn Consulting staff for stating at one event, "I hate people," which ironically made her one of our most beloved clients.

When she began working with me, she had many employees, but they were not managed. She hired them, trained them to her standards by giving them verbal instructions for a few days, followed with reminder post-it notes on cupboards in her catering kitchen; then she left them on their own to do the job. She expected them to understand the instructions from their initial training, then execute those standards with no follow-up, no continuing instruction, and no accountability (i.e. no leadership).

A similar scenario played out at her company's catering events. The employees competed with each other for top dog status, without input from Melanie. The winner of the top dog competition bossed everyone else around and ran the event to his/her own liking. To add to Melanie's problems, the top dog at the time happened to be her brother.

> Neglecting your employees is one of the most common mistakes that business owners make.

Melanie was understandably very frustrated with her team and frustrated with her business. She was playing small in leadership because she wasn't playing at all. There was no leadership system in her company beyond the initial training.

I am happy to report that Melanie completely turned her leadership around. She set up her standards, started having weekly meetings with her team, and created video trainings for every task in her business, from how to shred cheese to how to wash a pan. She set up a series of checks and balances between team members to ensure compliance with the standards, and even fired her brother. There were some tears mixed in with the growth required to make the changes, but Melanie is now playing BIG in leadership.

Neglecting your employees is one of the most common mistakes that business owners make. We are going to set up your employee management system later in this chapter which will almost eliminate your employee problems; and by "employee problems" I really mean bad management of employee problems.

Another common pitfall of playing small in leadership is illustrated through my client Julia's experience. Julia is a very gifted music teacher. She can teach a client to play an instrument in an hour. Seriously. Clients who have invested in music classes for years progress more in one course from her than from years of traditional music instruction.

Julia's business was growing rapidly. She needed to hire team members to run her sales, her marketing programs, and her teaching staff. Julia opted into my coaching program and came to an event afterward with a complaint. "I have a system for hiring now, but I can't get employees to stick around for more than a month. They all quit, and I have no idea why. I can't grow my business without a team, and I can't seem to grow my team."

As fate would have it, one of my neighbors, Shannon, applied for Julia's teaching position. Shannon was also a gifted musician and teacher, and was looking forward to joining Julia's team. Shannon was hired on, and I was thrilled for both of them.

It only took a few days before Shannon started reporting to me that all was not well in Julia's paradise. Shannon said that Julia had provided no clear cut direction for what she was to do as an employee, and that Julia asked her regularly how she should run her business. Julia had asked Shannon to train her (the business owner) on how to do her job after she (the employee) had figured it out. Nothing was in writing, and every detail from what the job would entail to how she would do it were constantly in flux.

Shannon was confused about what her position was, didn't know how to perform her mystery job to any standard, and didn't want the pressure of having to figure out how to run a business on top of doing her job. Shannon gave Julia the inevitable two-weeks' notice and moved on to a more stable, predictable work environment.

Julia's mistake in leading was that she was trying to make her employees act like business partners. Business partners (i.e. entrepreneurs) expect to create the business processes themselves, and are happy to change things on a regular basis until something works. As entrepreneurs, we live and breathe in the space of creation and change.

The employee mindset is very different from that of an entrepreneur. Your employees want stability and certainty. That is why they want to work for you, and they are not out creating their own businesses. They are probably more sane than you and I. They don't want to figure it out for themselves, and they want guaranteed results. They want to be told what to do, how to do it, to what standard it will be done, when it needs to be done, and they want recognition for doing a job well done. They want to follow someone else's path, and need to trust that the path has already been blazed for them. They are looking for a leader.

If you treat your employees as business partners, asking them to take part in creating the business with you, your employees will feel as if they are going on a hike into uncharted territory with a blind tour guide. They will inevitably decide they don't trust you enough to go on that hike with you, and they will put in their two-weeks' notice again and again and again.

> Don't expect your employees to act like entrepreneurs. A team of true employees is much more useful to you than a team of entrepreneurs.

Sometimes as entrepreneurs we get so excited about the business creation process that we think everyone has an affinity for taking big risks and jumping into the unknown like we do. They don't. Don't expect your employees to act like entrepreneurs. A team of true employees is much more useful to you than a team of entrepreneurs. They follow directions! They do what you ask! And here is the crux of it all--they want to follow you!

Instead of expecting water to come from a rock, let's accept that our employees are rocks, and give them what they need from us:

1. Security: A path carved out for them. This looks like a system. What do they do every day, every week, and every month in their position? What are the tasks they do and when do they do them? They are of course able to give input for improvements along the way, but they need the basic path carved out. We will build this system at the end of the chapter.

2. Direction: Someone to lead them on the path. This looks like guidance from a leader in the form of regular interaction in a predictable pattern (i.e. weekly meetings) as well as one-on-one time with their manager to hear them out and give them feedback. We will build a system for this as well.

3. Recognition: Acknowledgment that they are on the right path.

This looks like having standards in place so they know (and you know) when they have been successful. Most employees need to hear from their leader that they are on the right path as well. And you guessed it; this will be part of the leadership system.

Let's add to our list of common leadership mistakes before we begin creating that system for your employees. We have already discussed the first two.

LEADERSHIP MISTAKE #1
No structured training or management meetings

LEADERSHIP MISTAKE #2
System and standards not in place for employees

Here is our next mistake:

LEADERSHIP MISTAKE #3
Hiring friends and family.

When business owners look around for their first employee, their tendency is usually to go in the path of least resistance, i.e. skipping the recruiting phase and going straight into the hiring phase.

My client John has a successful contracting business. He is a brilliant builder, but isn't naturally gifted at keeping things organized, and his office was a disaster. He decided to hire an assistant. A woman at his church happened to approach him the next day and asked him if he had any job openings. He came to our next coaching call delighted with how easy it was to find an office assistant.

I had to ask. "Does she have previous experience working as a receptionist for a contractor?". You already know his reply. "She doesn't have any, but she is really excited about the job and willing to learn anything. I would also love to help her out. I know her family has been struggling, and I would love to work with someone from my church."

I continued. "Let's take heart and enthusiasm out of the decision making process for now, and just think logically. She has no previous experience. She just failed the first test of getting hired. Let's try the second."

I went on to explain, "The second test is this: if she were unable to perform the job to your company's standards, and you knew that if you fired her any of the following would happen:

1. suffer from a financial crisis because of the job loss
2. resent and blame you
3. cause a division between your mutual acquaintances
4. continue to be in your life in an uncomfortable way long after she worked for you

Would you still be able to fire her?"

> When business owners look around for their first employee, their tendency is usually to go in the path of least resistance, i.e. skipping the recruiting phase and going straight into the hiring phase.

Bob thought about that for a week. The next time we talked he had wisely placed a job listing on a job board, and advised the woman from his church to go through the application process.

Several weeks later he was raving about the woman he ended up hiring. "I had no idea I could find someone so perfectly suited for the job! She has experience working as an assistant for a builder, and already knows most of the job!"

When you are faced with the decision of choosing something easy in the beginning (i.e. hiring friends or family), please know that there is a decent to good chance that you will have to fire them or lay them off. Again, ask yourself: if you knew that any of the following would happen, would you be able to fire them anyway:

1. they will suffer from a financial crisis because of the job loss
2. they will resent and blame you

3. it will cause a division between your mutual acquaintances, especially if it is family

4. they will continue to be in your life in an uncomfortable way long after they work for you

I have broken the no friends and family rule in my own business from time to time. I have employed several family members and friends through the years with mixed results. I didn't want to fire my cousin. My business standards required it anyway. I didn't want to lay off my good friend. My lack of business profits at the time required it anyway. I didn't want to decrease my friend's sales commissions. My company's health required it anyway.

> I didn't want to fire my cousin. My business standards required it anyway.

If you could do the same, you have my blessing to hire friends and family.

LEADERSHIP MISTAKE #4

Putting employees (mostly low performing ones) ahead of company goals

I was on a call with a client a while ago named Kay. Her family owns a retail tire business that was hanging on by a thread. Kay constantly complained about her sole salesperson who continuously did not sell to the standards of the position. In fact, not only was the salesperson losing sales that should have been easy, he was talking people out of purchasing tires. My clients have dubbed this phenomenon un-closing sales.

With no extra capital to put into the business, we determined that replacing this one employee would be the first and most significant move to increase profits. Kay met with me for a two-hour intense session where we mapped out the standards for the new employee, scripted the conversation of letting the old employee go, and even wrote the job description, job listing, and interview questions for the new employee.

On our next call together I was expecting good news.

Kay started in. "I posted the ad and got ten good applicants. Two of them seemed great on the phone and I was so excited to interview them. But then I got to thinking about the new employee. If the company fails, I won't feel good about hiring someone, telling them the position will be long-term when the company might fail. I think I will just stick with our current salesperson until I know if the business will fail or not."

I don't make this stuff up. This is an actual conversation I had, bless her heart.

I explained that she would be, in fact, ensuring company failure if she didn't make the change.

That's when the truth came out. "I don't want to let my salesperson go. He has worked with us for a long time. I like him. He depends on this job, and he is always friendly and polite. It would crush him if I fired him."

She was willing to sacrifice her entire business to avoid having a hard conversation. She was willing to overlook her company goals to protect one employee's feelings.

> A business isn't a social gathering and it isn't a charity project. A business is a vehicle to serve the client.

This is one topic I can get fired up about. I kind of lit into her. "A business isn't a social gathering and it isn't a charity project. A business is a vehicle to serve the client. If you are serving your client effectively, you will have profits that will also serve you and your employees. If you are running your business as a social gathering or a charity project you will make decisions that are not about serving your client, and you will not have profits that will also serve you and your employees."

I continued, "What is most important to you: trying to please someone who isn't doing his job to standard or making that hard decision, having a hard conversation, and keeping the financial health of your business and your ability to serve your client to the best of your ability as THE priority?"

She listened quietly, so I kept going. "If you had a large business with large profits, you could easily afford some dead wood in your employees. If you are a small business with hairline profits, you don't have any room for dead wood in your business. You need to squeeze out every drop of performance from everyone on your team. You will need to let people go when they don't perform up to standards. It is time to grow a pair."

Okay, maybe I really didn't tell her to grow a pair, but I wanted to.

Think about your business. What standards are you letting slide because you are too afraid to have those difficult conversations? Do you realize that you are, in the end, hurting yourself, your customers, and your sub-standard employee by not ensuring the standards are being met? We will build these standards at the end of this chapter, but you will need to step up, face the fear of being bold, and enforce those standards.

LEADERSHIP MISTAKE #5
The Fren-ployee

What is a fren-ployee you may ask? A fren-ployee is a mix of a friend and an employee.

Just in case you think I am a goddess of business and don't make mistakes, this next scenario is about me.

One of my first employees, who I hired when I was the tender age of 24, was a college student named Barbie. At age 20, Barbie was only four years my junior, and I was a stay-at-home mom looking for a friend. I invited Barbie to stay after our first training together to have dinner with my family. I still remember sitting on the back patio eating hamburgers with her, and listening to her gush about how cool I was to have as a boss. I let myself get sucked in, and set myself up for failure.

For the next six months, I played frenployee with her and another member of my team. We talked about our marriages, our struggles, our hopes and dreams. We laughed about experiences at work. Everything was peachy until I promoted someone else (not Barbie) to manager.

> A good rule of thumb is to treat your employees as you would your best clients. We are always kind, friendly, open for conversation, but we don't move into that friend space.

She was furious and felt betrayed. We were such good friends! In her eyes I should have let her know who I was going to promote and why, and it should have been her. After all, that is what a friend would do. She was expecting me to operate by friend standards, because that was the role that I had been playing.

The final straw for her was when I discussed her performance with the new manager. As a friend, she felt that as a huge betrayal. She wrote me a long email with expletives and threatened to report me to the Better Business Bureau.

Maybe I should have been reported to the BBB; not for violating business standards, but for being a truly awful manager.

I hear many business owners who struggle with frenployee syndrome say, "I'm just too nice. I like people too much. I want to be their friend!" This is going to sound harsh, but you aren't too nice. You are too weak.

If you are trying to get your confidence from your employees telling you that you are cool, and telling you they like you, I am going to ask you to get your coddling needs met outside of your business.

A good rule of thumb is to treat your employees as you would your best clients. We are always kind, friendly, open for conversation, but we don't move into that friend space. Friend space looks like:

1. Going to them with personal problems
2. Asking them about personal issues
3. Hanging out with them outside of work

If you have already crossed that line, it is time for a conversation. Here is my Dr. Phil version of how this conversation would go:

"Hi (employee's name). I know that in the past we have blurred our working relationship with our friendship, but I can't continue having one foot in the manager role and one foot in the friendship role. I value your friendship, but I have to act more like a manager from now on. What that means is I will no longer be talking about my personal problems with you, and I won't be able to hang out with you outside of work. It might be awkward at first, but I hope you'll be able to stick it out with me and move into a healthy working relationship."

If your employees are your best friends and you want to keep it that way, make sure they know that given the choice, you will put the health of your business above the rules of friendship as needed.

Whenever I choose to work with friends, I make a decision ahead of time to play by the following rules: when a conflict arises (and I can guarantee that a conflict will eventually arise), I will make my decision based on what is best for my business, and make the same decision

I would make if the conflict involved another one of my employees. Many friends, like Barbie, won't be able to understand the different roles you need to play, and there is a good chance you will hurt feelings, and possibly lose friendships. If you play with frenployee fire, there is a good chance one of you will get burned.

LEADERSHIP MISTAKE #6
Not enforcing standards

The next mistake is compounded when you have fren-ployees. It is often hard to enforce standards with your friends.

Think back to your high school days. Who was your favorite teacher? Who was that teacher you learned the most from?

Chances are that teacher was pretty strict. You may have had to study more for that teacher than any other teacher.

My favorite teacher was Mrs. Melrose. She looked very old to me when I was 16 (she was probably 60). I walked into her room on the first day of class and saw little Mrs. Melrose in her brown wool suit, with a giant pair of rose-colored glasses perched on her nose, and I whispered something disrespectful about her to my friend.

I soon realized I had underestimated her. Mrs. Melrose earned my respect the minute she opened her mouth. "Sit down right now. We don't have any time to waste. We are going to go through a journey of history, and we have a lot to cover. Put your text books under your desks; you won't be using them because they are a waste of time. I don't tolerate any talking out of turn, and I don't tolerate any disrespect in my classroom. Are there any questions?"

> With the new rules of we-do-just-the-fun-stuff, the game would end quickly. There was no challenge, no standard to follow, nothing to test themselves against.

Mrs. Melrose took us through a whirlwind that year of making history, politics, and even law come to life. I had to work hard to earn an A in her classes, and sometimes I didn't. She challenged me to push myself. She was the inspiration behind my desire to become a teacher.

How different my experience was in her classroom than with different teachers with a softer approach. I knew that Mrs. Carey the biology teacher would let me retake any test I wanted to if I asked. I knew my physical science teacher would increase my grade just by talking to her about the test after class. I knew I could do the homework for my chemistry class in class, during Mr. Fifer's lecture. I wasn't inspired in any of these classes, and I didn't challenge myself to grow.

The same principle applies to your business. Employees are looking to you as a leader for much more than a good time. They want to be challenged. They want the bar to be set, and raised, and raised again. They want to know that they personally are capable of doing great things. By your maintaining that standard, and their reaching it, they in turn feel good about themselves. That is your role as a leader.

When my kids were very young, they liked to play Candy Land. They would follow the rules for a while, drawing out a red square and moving to a red square, and every once in a while drawing out a special candy card and moving to the Molasses Swamp or the Peanut Brittle Forest. Almost without fail, my kids would eventually want to go through the stack of cards and pull out just the special candy cards. They wanted to play the game without standards or rules.

With the new rules of we-do-just-the-fun-stuff, the game would end quickly. There was no challenge, no standard to follow, nothing to test themselves against. Because the rules had been removed, the game was no longer fun.

The same thing happens with your employees. If you run your business like social hour, your employees have nothing to test themselves against. Even though they may not realize it, they are wanting you to be strict. They want you to enforce those high standards, and they want to stretch to reach them. They want to feel accomplished.

We will build in a follow-up system for each standard that you set at the end of this chapter.

LEADERSHIP MISTAKE #7
Not Hiring Employees at all

The last leadership mistake is probably the most inhibiting. You simply cannot grow your business if you don't hire help.

You might have the same question that I am asked frequently when I am speaking on this topic. "How do I hire employees when I can't afford to hire employees?"

Think back to the day you launched your business. You invested money into inventory, a computer, and office supplies at a bare minimum. You invested this money with no promise of return on your investment, no sales coming in; all you had was a business plan and faith. But you did it anyway. You held your breath, took a step into the dark, and through some grit, determination, and a lot of hard work, you made it to where you are now.

> My job isn't to make your life easy. My job is to help you take your business to the next level.

You will have to exercise this faith each time you uplevel your business. When you are used to being a solopreneur, risking the money to hire an employee will feel uncomfortable and maybe even scary to you. All you will have is a growth plan and faith.

I challenge you to hold your breath, feel the fear, and do it anyway.

The reason I want you to hire out tasks in your business at this point is not to make life easier for you. I wish that were the case, but my job isn't to make your life easy. My job is to help you take your business to the next level. The reason I want you to hire things out is so you can spend more time on tasks that grow your business. I want you to spend more of your time on leadership and marketing. Spending your time in these two areas is the most important time you can spend as a business owner.

Here are your action steps for this chapter:

- Write a list of all employees, and which problems you are having with each of them

- You will take action on this list in the next chapter

CHAPTER 9

YOUR EMPLOYEE TASK SYSTEM

I hope that you are seeing the importance of systematizing your leadership. This section of the book will separate the students of business from the doers of business. You can't succeed if you never start DOING. Your temptation will be to skip over this section of the book, and move on to reading more theory. Please don't do that. Get out your laptop, and let's build this system right now. If you come to my Business Intensive Retreats, we will build a comprehensive Plug & Play Business System at the retreat. In this book, we will build a simplified version of several pieces of the Plug & Play system.

The first thing you will need to do is create a new spreadsheet and entitle it LEADERSHIP. Create a separate tab or worksheet for every employee on your team.

You will treat yourself like an employee of the business. Create a spreadsheet for yourself as well, as an employee of your business. As an employee of your own business, you will not be able to

> Your temptation will be to skip over this section of the book, and move on to reading more theory. Please don't do that. Get out your laptop, and let's build this system right now.

hire out your work in the future unless you have determined what exactly you do!

I recommend keeping tasks associated with each "hat" in your business together. The hats of business are: leadership, marketing & sales, product development, customer service & fulfillment, and finance. When you are ready to hire your first person, give them all of the tasks in one of those hats. You will slowly hire out all of the hats except for leadership, which will always belong to you.

After recording the name of each employee (and that might just be you) at the top of the worksheet, the next thing you will do is divide the worksheet into two sections: regular, continuing tasks on the top, and one-time tasks on the bottom. You will then set up the following column headers for both the regular and the one-time tasks:

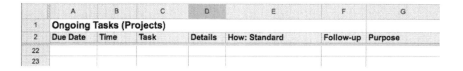

	A	B	C	D	E	F	G
1	Ongoing Tasks (Projects)						
2	Due Date	Time	Task	Details	How: Standard	Follow-up	Purpose
22							
23							

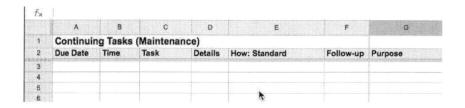

	A	B	C	D	E	F	G
1	Continuing Tasks (Maintenance)						
2	Due Date	Time	Task	Details	How: Standard	Follow-up	Purpose
3							
4							
5							
6							

Continuing tasks are things that are done on a regular basis in your business. For example, your business probably posts on social media daily. This would go in the continuing tasks section.

One-time tasks are exactly that--things you do once, then never again. Designing the home page on your website is a one-time task, until you update it in three years and it is again added to your one-time task list.

You are going to brain dump all of the tasks your business does on a regular basis (maintenance) and all of the tasks that your business needs to do just once (one-time tasks). Take your time and make this list complete. Then divide up which tasks are yours, and which tasks belong to each employee.

Now that you have a very long task list for each person, and you have placed continuing tasks at the top of your worksheet and one-time tasks at the bottom, you are ready to fill out the rest of this spreadsheet.

Due date:
You will record the date each task is due. This will not be a start date on a project; it will be the actual due date. Break down any big task into one-hour or less micro tasks. If you do this, the start date for the project will be the same as the due date.

You will have many more tasks than can be completed in one day. You will need to assign different due dates to your tasks. I recommend no more than three tasks assigned to a day.

Time:
Record how long that task is expected to take. If you write 15 minutes in this column, the employee gets a good sense of how long you expect that task to take. I have seen employees take hours on a project that was expected to take 15 minutes, simply because they weren't given direction on how long it should take them.

Task:
Write down each specific task that the employee will do. Get as detailed as possible. Each task should take no longer than one hour to complete, and should be able to be checked off a list. These are your micros. Tasks include the actual TASK required, not the GOAL of the task. Another word for GOAL would be a MACRO, as you learned in the last chapter.

Everyone likes to talk about goals. You can probably hear your mom's voice in your head saying, "Set goals every year. Write your goals down and you are 78% more likely to achieve them!" You can also create a vision board with your goals. I probably love goal setting as much as your mom, but setting a goal is only the first step.

Goals sound something like this:

- Get new clients
- Get PR exposure
- Start a marketing plan
- Have a following on Facebook

The problem with setting just goals is that they aren't an action plan. We don't know what we are DOING to get these results. Goals are not tasks.

We are going to set goals each month, then quickly move into the world of tasks.

Here are some good TASK examples. I want you to choose tasks that can be completed in one hour or less, and can be checked off a list. Notice that these tasks correspond to the goals listed above, but are actually executable steps instead of just lofty dreams.

- Sign up for trade show in NY for August
- Write a press release about new gadget and send to Julie from the Phoenix Times
- Purchase Kim's retreat so I can create my marketing plan
- Create Facebook ad

Details:
The next column on the spreadsheet that you are creating is the DETAILS. Use this column to record more details about the task, including websites, contact information, etc.

Standard:
Now comes the critical part when you are working with employees. You will write a STANDARD for every regular task on their list.

It is not an employee's job to guess your head. He/she needs to know exactly how you want the job done, when you want it done, what you want done, and to what standard of completion you want it done. Here are some examples of standards for the tasks we used before.

- Sign up for trade show in NY for August
- STANDARD: Pay no more than $700 for a booth. Purchase using the American Express card. Choose a booth near the front entrance, and preferably on a corner.

- Write press release about new gadget and send to Julie from the Phoenix Times
- STANDARD: Follow the press release template I emailed you. Send to me to approve before sending to Julie.

- Purchase Kim's retreat to create my marketing plan
- STANDARD: Go to www.womensbusinessretreat.com. Use the company credit card. Schedule for the next retreat with openings.

- Create Facebook ad
- STANDARD: Use template I have emailed you. Choose attention-grabbing picture. Send to me to approve before running ad

As you may have noticed, including the standard requires much more work on the management end. It requires you to think through the problems that may arise when doing each task, and eliminate questions and problems before they come up. Writing standards may single-handedly eliminate the putting-out-fires culture in your business and move it to a more peaceful, proactive way of running your business. This alone could change your life.

Follow-up:

Just when you thought I made you do enough work as a manager by writing out standards for each task, now I am going to ask you to pre-determine how you will follow-up with each task. I hope you are grasping that the time invested on the front end of leadership prevents the negative stuff from happening on the back end. I am a strong believer in the phrase, "An ounce of prevention is worth a pound of cure." In this case, five minutes spent planning is worth an hour of putting out fires.

> Writing standards may single-handedly eliminate the putting-out-fires culture in your business and move it to a more peaceful, proactive way of running your business. This alone could change your life.

I recommend that you follow up on every task you ask your employees to do for the first two weeks of their employment. Yes, two weeks. You can have them email you when it is completed, call you with a report of their day every day, or if they work next to you, check in with them every hour to ensure everything is done to standard. It will be a pain in the butt, and you will think it is overkill, but if you can train them early that you mean business following the standards, they will follow them for the rest of their employment with you.

Here are some sample follow up procedures to go with our examples:

- Sign up for trade show in NY for August
- FOLLOW-UP: put it on my calendar when it is booked

- Write press release about new gadget and send to Julie from the Phoenix Times
- FOLLOW-UP: already built in when your employee emails you for approval

- Purchase Kim's retreat to create my marketing plan
- FOLLOW-UP: email me with the date of the retreat when you finish

- Create Facebook ad
- FOLLOW-UP: already built in when your employee emails you for approval

PURPOSE:
The next column on your spreadsheet is PURPOSE. The reason we list a purpose for employee tasks is to help them understand the bigger picture. Employees often only see their side of the business, and don't realize that other positions in the company have different needs. If an employee is balking at a task, questioning the usefulness of a task, or just not getting it done on time or done correctly, there is a good chance they don't understand the purpose

of the task. I always list the purpose of each task the employee does on a regular, repeated basis and only list the purpose on a one-time task if I foresee them questioning its importance.

Here are some sample purposes:

- Sign up for trade show in NY for August
- PURPOSE: we get 200 leads at every trade show

- Write press release about new gadget and send to Julie from the Phoenix Times
- PURPOSE: we will probably be featured on their business page

- Purchase Kim's retreat so I can create my marketing plan
- PURPOSE: I need to learn how to run this business successfully

- Create Facebook ad
- PURPOSE: I want to grow my Facebook following to 10,000

Some of the purposes in these examples seem obvious and kind of stupid. You don't need to list a purpose for every task; just the ongoing tasks and the ones your employees are stalling or balking at.

Go ahead and create this spreadsheet right now, even if it takes a while. Seriously, now. If you think you will come back to this after reading the rest of the book, you won't. You will essentially have to re-read the entire book, and if you think you will do that later, you won't. Do it now. Go get your computer and set up this spreadsheet.

Write out every task each employee does on a regular basis, including yourself, the time it should take them, the standard for the task, and how you follow up. Then write down all of the one-time tasks (projects) you need to

> Go ahead and create this spreadsheet right now, even if it takes a while. Seriously, now. If you think you will come back to this after reading the rest of the book, you won't.

do, and the rest of your employees need to do. If you need help building out your employee tasks and standards, please come to a Business Intensive Retreat where we walk you through each step of setting this up.

Here are your action steps for this chapter:

- Create an employee tracker for each position in your company
- Start with the next position you want to hire out

CHAPTER 10

THE 3-STEP LEADERSHIP SYSTEM

Now that we have created your Employee Task System, we can just expect our employees to run the system without needing any more interaction from us, right?

Wrong.

Employees are human. They are not robots. They need a little more attention from you to stay happy in their job. And when they aren't happy in their job, following the DWM (Daily, Weekly, Monthly) Leadership System that I am about to teach you will allow you to keep them happy and/or plan for their replacement before they give their two-weeks' notice.

As with any good system, the DWM Leadership System requires more work from you upfront to eliminate work for you on the back end. It is the hard-to-easy principle. We are going to do some hard work upfront to make the future easy. Unsuccessful leaders follow the easy to hard principle. They do the easy thing upfront (i.e. not meeting with their employees regularly) which makes the future hard (i.e. employees quitting or causing drama). A good leader follows the hard-to-easy principle. They do the hard things now to make the future easier.

The first step, the DAILY step, of the DWM Leadership System is to have the employees meet with you or report to you every day for the first two weeks of work. If they work in an office with you, they will come into your office and you will together walk through the Employee Task System spreadsheet to ensure everything was done on time and to standard. If they work remotely, they will email in their tasks for the day.

A good leader follows the hard-to-easy principle. They do the hard things now to make the future easier.

Step two of the DWM Leadership System, the W, stands for, you guessed it, Weekly. You will meet with all of your direct reports for a weekly management meeting. The meeting is held at the same time and place every week, and is mandatory to attend. If you have more than five direct reports, it is time to place a middle manager or a team leader in between you and the masses. Five is the magic number of direct reports; any more than that and you usually aren't able to manage effectively.

When you get to that point, you will have your middle manager or team leader create an Employee Task System for every person on his or her team as well.

The weekly meeting is a chance for you to get the entire team on the same page with big projects. Remember those MACRO projects we talked about earlier? The weekly meeting is a chance to review the progress on all of those MACRO projects. I also like to hear number reports at each meeting, as shown in the example below. Whatever is reported in the weekly meetings is what your employees will naturally focus on during the week. I have found the phrase, "Whatever you track, grows" to be true.

Here is a sample weekly meeting agenda format:

1. MACRO project reporting from each team member

2. Numbers reports from each team member. Examples include:

- How many leads

- How many sales
- How much income the ad dollars spent produced
- How many clients signed up
- How many hits to the website
- How many opt-ins
- How many customers came in the door, etc.

3. Goals for the numbers from each team member. These could be a monthly number goal they are trying to reach, or a weekly goal. Included with this is a plan for how to increase the numbers they are trying to hit.

4. Celebration & Request. Each team member states a celebration they had for the week. This is the human part of management--it feels wonderful to celebrate and be recognized for successes! This is also their chance to make requests from you or anyone else on the team. Sometimes requests are specific things like, "I need you to rewrite that email autoresponder by Tuesday," and sometimes requests are more generic. "I need extra compassion and understanding this week." This is your employees' chance to tell you what they need.

We are through the first two steps of the DWM Leadership System. If you only did these first two steps you would eliminate or prevent most management problems. We aren't going to stop there though. We are hard-core business owners, and we take our businesses seriously. We are going to move on to the magic third Monthly step, asking the 7 Magic Questions in the monthly private interview.

> If you only did these first two steps you would eliminate or prevent most management problems.

I usually hold monthly private interviews either before or after each weekly meeting so I can fit my entire team into the schedule each month. We again meet at the same time and place each month so it is systematized; once it is set up, you will never have to think about it again.

You will record the answer to each of the 7 Magic Questions as your employee answers them. This is an interview; it is not appropriate for you to be talking much in this interview. You talk enough. This is your chance to listen to your employee.

Asking your employee to go against that culture and tell you what they really think may not be easy for them at first.

Here are the 7 Magic Questions in the order you will ask them. Ask them these same Magic Questions every month.

1. What is working for you? (you, meaning the employee)

The employee will tell you what they like about their job and what is working well. If they give you the answer, "Everything," ask them to give you specifics. You will record what they say on a spreadsheet next to the date. Your only response should be something like, "That's great." Again, this is your time to listen.

2. What is working for me? (me, meaning yourself)

Now is your time to talk. Give them 3-5 specific things they are doing well. If you tend to speak in generalities (i.e. you are doing a great job) take the time to write out 3-5 things ahead of time that show you they are doing a great job. These could be things like:

- I appreciate that you are always on time
- You write detailed emails so I know exactly what is going on
- You greet our customers immediately when they walk in the door
- You are quick to respond to my emails

This is pretty standard stuff so far, but this interview is about to become a bit tougher.

3. What is not working for you? (you, meaning the employee)

Your employee is probably not used to being asked for his/her opinion on things. Our educational system sets up a culture that says the boss/teacher is in charge and is not to be questioned. Asking your employee to go against that culture and tell you what they really think may not be easy for them at first. You may get some answers like, "Nothing. Everything is great."

You get to dig deep as a manager and persist. I like this phrase: "If there were something that wasn't working for you, what would it be?"

> This isn't about the problem itself; this is about empowering your employees to become fixers-of-the-problems.

Then sit and wait, even if it takes ten minutes of them hemming and hawing. Eventually you will get a meek answer with a lot of apologies that sounds something like this. "Well, this isn't a big deal at all, and it really is fine, but . . . " and that is when the gold comes out of their mouth. You just gave them permission to have a voice, and have influence and ownership in their position. You just gave them job satisfaction and validation. Yeah! Celebrate that!

Your natural reaction to hearing a problem in your business is then going to be to jump in and defend it or fix it. You will resist. You are going to move on to the next Magic Question.

4. What are some possible solutions that you see to fix this problem? (you, meaning the employee)

If you get an "I don't know" answer, you will need to exercise patience. Sure, you can help them brainstorm solutions, but don't you dare take control and fix their problem for them! This isn't about the problem itself; this is about empowering your employees to become fixers-of-problems. With a team of problem-solvers instead of quiet martyrs suffering in silence, you will eliminate most of your management problems and create a culture in which your employees feel ownership and love their jobs. It really does work. That is why they are called the 7 MAGIC Questions!

We are now moving on to the hardest question that you will address in this interview.

5. What is not working for me? (me, meaning you)

This is your chance to give specific, detailed feedback to your employee. Even if your employee is quasi-perfect, this is your chance to dig deep and let them know extremely specific things they could do to improve. I usually only focus on one thing that needs improvement at a time, so pick your top concern if you have many. This will sound something like this:

"I have noticed that you have come late to our last three management meetings. I feel unvalued when you come late. It also throws off our meeting schedule when we wait for you. What are some possible solutions you see for fixing this?"

Notice that I gave the feedback in this format:

a. Name the behavior, without judgment or exaggeration. Just state the facts as they are. "I have noticed that you have come late to our last three management meetings."

b. Name your feelings. When you say the phrase "I feel LIKE . . . " you are no longer naming feelings. "I feel like you don't care about this business" is an accusation, not a feeling statement. Stick with feeling words: unappreciated, unvalued, troubled, sad, etc. The more vulnerable the feeling, the more disarming it will be for the employee. Vulnerability works. If your feeling word fits into this phrase: "I feel (word) AT/WITH YOU," you are moving into blaming. Blaming words like disappointed, angry, frustrated sound like you are attacking, and aren't vulnerable. Sharing attack feelings will backfire and will prevent the open conversation that you are looking for from happening.

If the relationship is so deteriorated that you can't bring yourself to use a vulnerable feeling word, skip the feeling part entirely rather than throw in a blaming word.

The reason we use a feeling word is to remind employees that we are human. Even though we are the boss, we still have feelings. This usually softens your employees to let their guard down when they have seen that you have let yours down.

c. The third part of this conversation, after you have named the behavior and shared your feelings about it, is to name the natural consequences that are already happening because of

their behavior. In the example above, the natural consequence was, "It also throws off our meeting schedule because we wait for you." We again give the state of the union--we just tell things as they are. Keep all blaming words and accusations out of this. It may feel good to you to pour on the guilt and make them suffer, but it makes the problem worse. Go punch a few walls or whine to your spouse if it makes you feel better, but don't make this conversation about you or your desire to punish anyone. This conversation is a time to practice problem-solving instead of punishing.

d. Ask for their solutions. "What are some possible solutions you see to fixing this?" Notice that we ask our employees to solve their own problems, as well as the problems we have with them.

I love the visual of never letting an employee come into your office with a problem without also ensuring they are taking that problem out of the office with them when they leave. The same goes for your problems that you are having with them. You give it to them, and they take it out of the office with them. It is theirs to solve.

Your natural inclination will probably be to rescue your employee. Watch yourself saying things like, "It really isn't that big of a deal . . . I am sure I can figure out a way to work around it . . . " Bite your tongue and simply let them step up to the plate and find their own solution to this problem.

Another trap you might fall into is having these conversations with the entire group instead of during a one-on-one. Imagine this scenario: Lisa is frequently late to meetings. Instead of addressing it with her individually, you casually remind everyone in the weekly group meeting that they all need to be there on time. Everyone nods their head in agreement and you think the problem is solved. And then Lisa is late again.

When you try to solve an individual problem in a group setting there are two results. The perfect workers are usually over-accountable, taking everything you say to heart. They believe they are the ones that are being chastised for being late, and they feel horrified that they were late that one time, two years ago. They now think you are mad at them.

In the meantime, the employee that is causing the problem is usually the under-accountable type. They assume that you are talking about someone else, or assume that everyone is late on a regular basis so they don't really need to worry about it. Management-by-group can actually make a problem worse than if you didn't address it at all.

Assuming you had a one-on-one conversation with the employee, the next question you are probably asking me is "What if I do this, and the problem still doesn't get any better? What if she still comes late to the next meeting?"

> Put yourself in their shoes. After going through that, would they ever want to be late again?

It is time to immediately have a second sit-down with the employee, and follow this script:

"We just talked last week about being on time for meetings, and we came up with solution x. You were late today. What can you do to prevent this from happening again, and what will happen the next time you are late?"

Your employee would determine the consequence. Maybe he would be docked pay, maybe she would write a note of apology to everyone on the team whose time they are wasting, maybe he would get a formal write-up in his file. Let the employee brainstorm with you what those consequences would be.

Put yourself in their shoes. After going through that, would they ever want to be late again?

If the employee is not able to meet the standards for the third time, it is time to prepare to let the employee go if necessary. Go ahead and post the job, gather resumes, and be ready to start the hiring process.

You will sit down with your chronically tardy employee, go through the written series of interviews you have had with her to fix the problem, state that the problem has not been fixed and the employment arrangement is no longer working for you. It is best to have these conversations using the band-aid removal technique. Just come out and say it; no beating around the bush. The conversation will be very short.

By always tracking the conversations you have with your employees, you will protect yourself from disgruntled employees and potential lawsuits. To leave a very clear documented trail, it is a good idea to send an email copy after every one-on-one meeting you have with the employee, and ask for a confirmation email back saying they received it.

Now that we have addressed what you will do if things continue to go wrong, we are going to come back to the 7 Magic Questions. After you ask them to come up with solutions for what is not working for you, you will move on to question #6.

6. What is your goal for this month?

Once again, we let the employees take charge. He determines (with your approval) what he will be working on this month. Your employees will surprise you. They will want to work on background problems that you didn't even know existed. They will want to work on personal development skills like being more bold. They will want to develop a stronger working relationship with someone else on the team. Or they may just want to kick ass with their current goals. Stand back and watch them be amazing.

> The first time you ask your employees this one it will really stress them out. My employees tell me they stew over this question for days before their monthly interview.

One of the women on my team recently surprised me by setting a goal of learning all the basics of all of the positions in the company, so she could play backup in case of any emergency. I hadn't thought of that! Your employees have goals that you haven't thought of as well.

That leads us to our last, and my very favorite, magic question.

7. What is one thing I can do to manage you better?

The first time you ask your employees this one it will really stress them out. My employees tell me they stew over this question for days before their monthly interview. It is a serious dilemma: How do you tell your boss, the person that is in charge of your paycheck, that some things they do are really screwy? It is a fun question to ask!

Inevitably, some of your employees will try to weasel out of the question with something like this. "I really can't think of anything. I love working here and there isn't anything you could do differently. "

> The employee is never the problem. If an employee is behaving or performing poorly and the problem hasn't been addressed or the employee has been fired, you are the problem. Gulp.

When I hear that, I have a script that I use that works every time. Try it: "Every month I get to give you feedback which helps you grow in your position. If I didn't get any feedback from you, I would never get the opportunity to grow. This is my chance to get that feedback. Take a few minutes if you need to, but let me know what is one thing I can do to manage you better."

And then just stop talking and wait. I learned this trick when I was an English teacher. I would ask a question, then just stop and give the students lots of wait time. In my head I would simply say to myself, over and over again, "I am a teacher. I can wait forever." And I would. And it always works.

Sooner or later, your employee will cough out the following words. "Well, this really isn't a big deal at all, but if I had to think of something it would be . . . " and then you again get the truth. I have gotten the following feedback through the years: I change my mind too frequently, I forget decisions I have already made, I discount others' concerns, I micromanage things, and I hurt people's feelings when I second-guess their follow-through. And all of that feedback has made me a better manager!

The resistance to asking this question that you might be experiencing right now (and this resistance usually comes more frequently from men I might add) is that your employees, if given a voice, will no longer respect you as a manager and will take over.

All I can say is--I dare you. Try it and let me know about your experience. I have never seen anyone revolt because she was given a voice. The opposite is usually the truth.

So there you have it. The Employee Task System that requires you to set up your employees in their positions knowing exactly what they do, when they do it, and how they do it. You now have the DWM Leadership System that requires you to meet with your employees on a daily basis for the first two weeks, a weekly basis as a group, and a monthly basis individually. You also now have the 7 Magic Questions that will empower your employees with a voice and a sense of influence and purpose.

I hope you noticed along the way that all leadership problems begin and end with you. The employee is never the problem. If an employee is behaving or performing poorly and the problem hasn't been addressed or the employee hasn't been fired, you are the problem. Gulp.

Taking ownership of all employee problems also puts all of the power back into your hands as well. There is no need to beat yourself up for not having the training that you now have. You are responsible, however, for taking action on this training.

Here are your action steps for this chapter:

1. Finish creating all Employee Task System worksheets

2. Schedule and begin weekly management meetings

3. Schedule monthly private interviews an ongoing basis for all employees

4. Schedule an immediate private interview for any employee that needs behavior or performance adjustments

5. Dismiss any thoughts of guilt or shaming yourself for not already having done this. Repeat after me: guilt does not serve.

CHAPTER 11

PLAYING BIG IN CUSTOMER SERVICE

We were sitting in the upstairs training room in my family cabin, where the Business Intensive Retreats had their humble beginnings. I had just led the group of entrepreneurs through the Cash Quadrant System, a training that leads business owners to realize what actually makes them money in their businesses.

Eli was a smart guy. He was a divorce attorney, and he could play verbal judo with the best of them. He had an unparalleled vocabulary, asked intelligent questions, and also wasn't afraid to ask when he didn't understand. He raised his hand.

"So what you are saying is I am not making money when I am working with a client? But that is what I bill for. Whenever I work with a client I am making money."

"Think about it," I replied. "You only make money when that client gives you a check. When you are fulfilling on work for that client you aren't making money; you are spending time."

Eli looked stunned. "Holy Frijoles . . . this is going to change my whole business!"

Okay, maybe he didn't say "Holy Frijoles," but he was excited to realize that he didn't have to limit himself by trading time for dollars any more. This concept is new for many small business owners, especially professionals like lawyers, doctors, and dentists. When you can break out of employee mindset which says, "I am paid by the hour for the work I do," and move into business owner mindset which says, "I am paid by the results of my company," your world will change.

> When you can break out of employee mindset which says, "I am paid by the hour for the work I do," and move into business owner mindset which says, "I am paid by the results of my company," your world will change.

A few weeks ago, I took my 12-year-old daughter to several orthodontist offices for consults. I was pleasantly surprised at how the two offices showed the difference between employee mindset and business owner mindset so perfectly.

The first one I went to was a typical business-owner-as-employee setup.

There was of course a receptionist who greeted us and got our paperwork filled out. Then we were called back into a small room and talked to the orthodontist as he checked my daughter's teeth and gave his recommendations. He took one patient at a time, and there were a few people waiting in the waiting room. Standard procedure.

The next orthodontist visit was completely unexpected, as most professionals don't ever move into the business owner mindset. I was impressed!

As a systems girl, I recognize systems immediately when I see them. The receptionist not only gave the parents a clipboard to fill out, but gave the teenage patients one too. She then gave my daughter a bag of goodies and told her she could have one of the fresh-baked cookies on the tray when she was finished with the orthodontist. My daughter was already a fan.

I followed my daughter into the "back", expecting the obligatory small private room, and instead was surprised with a completely different format. I walked into a giant open room with floor-to-ceiling windows and lots of live plants. There were about 20 dental chairs in a circle around the room, with a dental assistant working over a patient in every chair. The orthodontist was on a stool with wheels, and was whirling around from patient to patient in an orchestrated dance. It was busy, but not chaotic. Every few minutes you would hear, "Doctor, code x in chair 12" and the orthodontist would smoothly wheel over to chair 12 for a peek into a mouth, a few words of instruction, and then was off to respond to the next soft call of "Doctor, code y in chair 4."

Yep, I hate to say it, but it was like a well-oiled machine. This doctor, with the help of his magnificent systems and well-trained staff, was working on 20 patients at a time instead of 1. Sure, he was paying a lot for staff, but would you rather be making 50% of 20, or 100% of 1?

Eli the lawyer took this to heart at the retreat, and has since hired on more workers to do the legal legwork for him, while he spends most of his time finding new clients. Leadership and marketing are the two most critical roles of the business owner; not customer service or fulfillment.

Inevitably, there is a downside with increased production. The inherent problem of scaling your business (serving people en masse instead of one at a time) is that you lose the human connection. That orthodontist doesn't know his patients. Eli isn't in court as much, practicing his verbal art.

> The inherent problem of scaling your business (serving people en masse instead of one at a time) is that you lose the human connection.

And that is why you, as the business owner, get to choose! If you absolutely love working with your clients, no one is going to hold a gun to your head and make you stop. You still get to do that. But maybe you need to hire out 90% of the fulfillment, and only work with the top 10% of your clients directly. Only the fantastic, best qualified ones. What sounds bad about that?

Eli recently returned to another Business Intensive Retreat. He asked me, "Why are you still running your own retreats? You could have trainers doing all of this for you. You could swing by and do a guest appearance on one night and call it good. Why are you here?"

> When presented with this balance game, many small business owners make a bizarre choice. They choose to spend their time doing things they don't enjoy, and don't make money either.

My answer? "Because I love it. I love being here. I love training. I have hired out almost everything else in my business, but I love these retreats."

And that is the beauty of being a business owner. You get to choose. If at times you would like to put your personal enjoyment of the job ahead of what is financially most profitable, you get to give yourself that permission.

When I hear clients say to me however, "Kim, I can't hire out what I do. No one can do it as well as I can. The clients are paying for ME," I know that they are not giving themselves permission. They are holding themselves in a lie that can become a hamster-wheel trap.

Using a System for your Clients

My goal for you is to come up with a good balance of what is financially profitable in your business and your enjoyment of your business. If you only chase money I am afraid you will end up working too much and not enjoying your life. If you only do what you want to do, chances are you won't be profitable.

When presented with this balance game, many small business owners make a bizarre choice. They choose to spend their time doing things they don't enjoy, and don't make money either. Instead of choosing between money or fun, they choose being broke while doing tedious tasks.

This trap most often is the business owner believing she has to work personally with every client. If you are still answering the company phone or answering customer emails and you have other employee positions hired, you have fallen into the tedious tasks trap. If you are spending more than 20% of your time working with clients in fulfillment, and you have other positions hired out, you have also fallen into this trap.

So how do you systematize your customers, you ask?

Here is the system.

1. Train your clients to rely on your systems instead of you.

If you switch your customer service policy mid-stream with existing customers, they won't like it. You get to decide if you move ahead anyway, knowing that some of them will be unhappy during the transition period, or if you want to implement a grandfather policy where you continue to interact with previous clients as you have in the past.

I usually like a time-limited grandfather policy. I would tell clients something like, "I have loved speaking with you personally each month about your order, but my company is growing and we have needed to change a few policies. All of our clients will now be ordering directly from the website and then emailing in with any questions. However, because you have been such a great customer for a long time, I would love to continue taking your order by phone for the next three months until you get used to the new system."

This usually softens customers enough not to be unhappy with the change in policy.

After you have laid out your new customer service policy, moving as much as possible to a completely automated system (i.e. an interactive website with questions answered via email) you are ready to go hard core with customer service.

My goal for you is that you never answer your phone again.

First of all, I realize that in some industries this wouldn't be possible or desired. But if you can find a way to cut down your phone calls by even 10%, you have bought yourself precious time and fewer interruptions in your day.

Here are the steps toward never answering your phone again:

1. Let your customers know about your new policies to make things automated

2. Record your outgoing message to something like this:

"Hi, you have reached Jill with Natural Essential Oils. I generally don't answer the phone unless I am expecting a call. The best way to reach me is by texting me at this number, or emailing me at jill@emailaddress.com. Thank you!"

And then practice crazy self-control to refrain from picking up your phone. Ever. Unless it is your spouse or child.

Your clients will learn very quickly how to reach you, and your phone will stop ringing. I started doing this almost two years ago and now I get only one to two calls a day. And I don't answer them.

So now you know how to stop client phone calls and interruptions. Now we need to put a system in place to manage your customer relationship in an automated way so they don't feel neglected and still get their needs met.

You will once again need to create a spreadsheet, and you will entitle it "Client Tracker." Create a field for your client's name and contact information, then record the steps each client needs to go through in the fulfillment process.

Here is an example for Jill from the Essential Oils company.

CLIENT TRACKER

	A	B	C	D	E
1	**CLIENT TRACKER**				
2	Client Name	Contact Info	Sent Start-up Email	Emailed Contract	Received Signed Contract
3	Amy Smith	amy@gmail.com	4/13/2015	4/15/2015	pending
4					
5					

You will write out every step that new clients needs to go through. Here are some common steps that you will need to do for new clients:

- send them contract
- send them welcome email
- schedule them for meetings
- get payment
- send satisfaction survey
- ask for referrals

Go ahead and create this spreadsheet right now. As before, if you dog-ear this page and tell yourself you will come back to this, you won't. Now is your chance. Log in to Google Drive, and create a new spreadsheet entitled "Client Tracker." I prefer Google Drive over Excel because there is no danger of losing your work if your computer is lost or crashes. I also like the sharing setting on Google Drive so every employee in your company can edit the document simultaneously. No more emailing the most current draft back and forth!

> Go ahead and create this spreadsheet right now. As before, if you dog-ear this page and tell yourself you will come back to this, you won't. Now is your chance.

Write out all of the steps you would like to take your clients through. If it is easier to start this with just new clients rather than bringing all existing clients into the system, that is fine for now. Just get started!

A Note of Caution: Don't Divorce Your Client

While I am extremely passionate about automating customer service, there must be a balance between your company's time and ensuring the customer is happy. Some business owners that I have worked with have taken the "Systematize Your Client" mentality too far into the realm of "Divorce Your Client."

You never want to sever all ties with your clients and no longer communicate with them. Your business will have a hard time surviving if this is your mentality. Jessie is a marketing consultant who automated her customer service into the Divorce Your Client realm.

Jessie's company provides an inexpensive re-branding service using labor from India. Her company's designs look nice and are affordable. So far, so good.

Unfortunately, her customer service was automated to the point of divorce. Her customers were instructed to submit an automated e-ticket from her website each time they wanted to discuss a revision in the re-branding process. They waited up to four days for a response from the e-ticket. There was no way to talk to a real human being, and there was no way to register a complaint.

When people were unhappy with the service and made enough noise, they got an email from Jessie justifying her company's policies. She was in the habit of handling customer service complaints by justifying herself and blaming the customer.

Luckily, Jessie was open to the conversation of change. She realized that she needed to create more happy customers, and she needed to admit when her company had done wrong and fix the problems instead of justifying them. She hired a customer service rep to answer the phone, and has a new, non-defensive script her customer service rep uses when things go wrong:

"I'm so sorry that was your experience! What can we do to make this right?" They then talk through a plan to make things right.

Notice that she isn't handling the customers herself (she has systematized the process), but she hasn't severed all ties either (she isn't divorcing them). She is in a healthy, customer relationship with them.

Tools I like to Automate Customer Service/Fulfillment:

Here are some tools I strongly recommend for customer management. You can also visit http://kimflynn.com/kim-recommends/business-services for a comprehensive list of the services and products that I use and recommend to manage your business.

1. The Plug & Play Business System. I created the Plug & Play over many years of running many different businesses. The Plug & Play is a productivity system with client tracking, sales tracking, and employee tracking built in. It is truly your entire business in one place. For training on the Plug & Play Business System, please attend a Business Intensive Retreat.

2. Rocket Lawyer. At the time of the writing of this book, I pay $100 per year for this service. I primarily use this service to e-sign documents. Instead of having to send contracts back and forth, requiring scanning and emailing back, I upload the contract to Rocket Lawyer and clients can simply sign via email. The service tracks all documents that are signed, eliminating the need for paper storage as well. www.rocketlawyer.com

3. Time Bridge. I use Time Bridge to schedule appointments without having to go back and forth with email. It syncs with my Google calendar, and I simply select three or four times that work for me, then send the invitation to my client, asking them to select the best time out of the times I have chosen. I schedule both in-person meetings and phone calls with this tool. www.timebridge.com

4. Check Appointments. If you need to schedule appointments frequently, and don't need to speak to your clients live to do so, I strongly recommend using a service like Check Appointments. The clients go to your site, and simply schedule themselves. It syncs to your Google calendar. I have seen appointment-heavy industries like salons use this tool with great success, but you will need to train your clients to use it!

You can also use this tool internally; my team uses it to set appointments with my coaches. www.checkappointments.com

5. Jing. How do you train your clients or your employees in the use of these tools? One of my favorite tools for training is Jing. It is a free tool that records screen shot videos. You can walk people through how to use a tool on your own screen while you talk. Jing allows videos up to five minutes long. For longer videos, try Snagit. Both products can be found at www.techsmith.com.

6. Survey Monkey. This free service allows you to send out surveys that your clients can answer anonymously. Go ahead--be brave enough to ask your clients what they really think!

Here are your action steps for this chapter:

- Record a new phone message and practice letting your phone ring

- Create your client tracker spreadsheet

- Set up a survey to send out to all past clients about your product/service

CHAPTER 12

PLAYING BIG IN PRODUCT

We are ready to dive into how to play BIG in your product. Please keep in mind that when I say "product" it doesn't have to mean a physical product. Many companies offer a service as their product. Some businesses, like retail stores, provide product as a service. Whether you provide a service or have a physical product, we are going to call them all "product."

We are going to talk about three common product mistakes. As we walk through these mistakes, please be willing to look at your business honestly instead of making excuses for your business. Often times I hear from clients, "Oh, but my business is different." Watch for that phrase to come up in your head as you read. Chances are that is an excuse.

Product Mistake #1
Neglecting the High-end Upsell

For about ten years I owned a tutoring business. We provided one product: a month of tutoring. Each month the company would send out invoices for clients to pre-pay for a month of tutoring. They all paid the same amount regardless of who fulfilled on the tutoring, or how many months they used our service.

Every few months in this business someone would call into the office and say, "I want the best service that you have. I don't care how much it costs, I just want the best that you have to offer." These clients were usually wealthy, and wanted to do everything they could for their child who was struggling.

Unfortunately for us, we only had one product. We had the monthly fee for tutoring and no way to give a higher priced, better service to the client who wanted more. My tutoring company was missing out on an opportunity to make more money. I could have created a six-month or twelve-month service plan. I could have created a higher-end program that involved interacting with the child's school. I could have charged more for more experienced tutors. I could have added on a special online program. I could have worked with very high-end clients myself. I could have partnered with a home-study course company to provide more books and materials. There are many, many options for creating a high-end upsell, and I didn't have any in place.

> Not only was my company missing out on bringing in more revenue, my clients were missing out on the level of service that they wanted.

Not only was my company missing out on bringing in more revenue, my clients were missing out on the level of service that they wanted. They wanted the security of knowing that their child was being taken care of in the highest way possible. By offering only one service, I wasn't able to give them the security they were looking for. No one wins if you don't provide the product that your client is looking for.

If you don't have a high-end product in place, it is time to take a brainstorming break. What are some possible upsells that you could offer to existing clients? What is a higher level product that you could offer as an additional choice to new customers?

Product Mistake #2
Playing Only in Product

Leslie was a healthy-living blogger who loved to create product. Her current product line-up included 16 individual CD's and audios about healthy eating, a manual on using essential oils at home, an online program about healthy parenting, a book on healthy healing, and a weekly webinar training program about healthy living. She had a lot of products available, but wasn't selling much.

One of the first times I met with Leslie, I asked her this question. "If you had to make $1000 this month, without an option of failure, how would you do that?" Her answer was very telling. She said, "I guess I would create another product." Her mistake is a common one. Unfortunately, products don't create revenue. Sales of product create revenue.

Her product line-up would have worked if she could drive traffic to a single platform to talk about each one of her products individually. She decided to make her weekly webinar her primary product, and sell her various other products at the end of each webinar. Now she drives all traffic to one destination: the low-cost weekly webinar. I love how simplicity is often what works best. Leslie learned how to drive all traffic to one core product, and then offer upsells and cross-sells after customers had already purchased her core product.

It is easier to see someone's mistake when that person isn't you. Be aware that the tendency to want to create new products instead of selling the products you already have runs rampant in the entrepreneurial space, and is especially prevalent in the expert or info-preneur space. Entrepreneurs are natural creators. We want to create! Isn't it funny that creation can hold us back from success?

Raise your hand and repeat after me, "I will not create another product until I have learned how to sell the product I already have in an automated, systematized, predictable way." You will learn the basics of the **SELLSUM** marketing system, a systematized marketing plan to take any product or service out of your driveway and into the marketplace in a later chapter.

Product Mistake #3
Creating a Product with No Demand

Women are beautiful creatures. We generally like to serve. We usually go into business for the greater good; to uplift, inspire, help, serve, beautify, and enrich the human experience.

Sometimes we forget that peace, love, and joy aren't sold on Amazon.com for a reason. It is hard to sell peace, love, and joy. Sometimes we don't realize that people would rather buy a new pair of shoes than peace, love and joy.

> Raise your hand and repeat after me, "I will not create another product until I have learned how to sell the product I already have."

As a women's business coach, I work with many women who are in the business of selling peace, love, and joy. They might be life coaches, healers, spiritual advisors, or energy workers. Clients come to me wanting to start a business to help new moms, or a business to help teens, or a business to help sufferers of abuse.

Please know that if you choose this line of work, you must research supply versus demand in your area. In my area in Salt Lake City, I can attend a business networking group of 50 people and meet five energy healers or life coaches. If you want to go into this type of business, I encourage you to thoroughly research your competition and your industry, and have a dynamite marketing plan that will make you stand out of the crowd.

You must make sure your product has a demand for it before you launch into a business.

If you find yourself with this dilemma, and you know that the supply for your industry far outweighs the demand, I would encourage you to look around at other options. What needs do you have, do your friends have, does your spouse have that requires a solution? Think specifics--you may not be able to sell peace, love, and joy directly, but many people build businesses on things that give you a slice of that; maybe a new twist on a meal planner that brings peace to busy lives, a training program on parenting that brings more love in families, or a new style of diaper bag that inspires joy in the owner.

Product Mistake #4
Forgetting the Experience

Another common product mistake that small business owners make involves the experience surrounding the product itself. My experience with Matt the hairdresser illustrates this perfectly.

I heard amazing things about Matt. Matt was the premier hair dresser in my state. He had won awards, styled celebrities, and was featured in the press. A friend of mine drove two hours with her mom every few months to go to his salon and get their hair cut by Matt.

The first time I sat in Matt's chair I understood why people drove for hours. He was one of those mid-fifties guys who is still--can I say it?--hot. He was flirty in that non-threatening European kind of way. After he spent two hours on my cut and color, casually flirting with me the entire time, I felt beautiful and absolutely loved my new hair. And I never went back. Why?

While I was in the chair getting my hair cut, a non-stop stream of people came through Matt's area in the salon. His daughter came to say hi and chat, then his daughter's boyfriend brought some supplies, then three women who used to work there dropped in, then a client came over to chat before her appointment.

> He was one of those mid-fifties guys who is still - - can I say it?- - hot. He was flirty in that non-threatening European kind of way.

I felt awkward sitting in the middle of a group of people listening in on all of the private conversations just over my head. Matt had forgotten about the customer experience.

I still go to Matt's salon, but now I go to a woman named Kim who works in the back stations who doesn't have celebrity status. Kim's haircuts haven't won awards, and she definitely doesn't flirt with me in a non-threatening European way, but the experience is better for me. I choose to get a non-award winning product because I get a higher quality experience. A business isn't all about the product!

Think about your product or service. Put yourself in your clients' shoes from the first interaction with you right until the last interaction with you. Walk through their full experience and ask yourself these questions:

What could you change?

What could you add?

What could you delete?

The goal isn't to overhaul everything you are doing. The goal is to make small changes whenever you see the opportunity to improve your client's experience.

When it comes to product, don't make the four deadly product mistakes. Don't forget the high-end upsell, don't forget that selling one product is more important than creating many, don't create a product that has no demand, and don't forget the entire client experience!

Tools I Recommend to Create Product

Macbook pro: If you are going to create videos or audios on a consistent basis in your business, whether as product or marketing pieces or both, your time spent editing and uploading these will suck a lot less if you use a Mac over a PC. I am a PC girl, but there simply is no comparison when it comes to video management and editing. Your Macbook Pro will come with iMovie to edit movies, and Garageband to edit audio.

Screenflow: I use Screenflow on my Mac to record screenshot videos. Screenflow allows you to record just the screen, or a small video of you in the corner with your screen. This is good for creating webinars that you can replay as needed, with your picture in the corner of the screen.

Here are your action steps for this chapter:

- Spend one hour researching your industry. What products are your competitors selling?

- Add a high-end upsell to your core product.

- Write out your customer experience, from the moment they meet you, through the purchase decision, through the fulfillment process. What could be systematized?

CHAPTER 13

PLAYING BIG IN FINANCE

This is not a book on business finance. You should be relieved when I say that, because while finance books are important, they aren't very exciting reads. Reading a business finance book is like trying to stay awake while my son tells me about his progress on Minecraft. Very hard to do.

That said, understanding your business finances is critical. My high-end clients spend three days at a Finance Academy Retreat just learning business finance even though it has almost killed some of them. It is important enough to risk death to learn the language of business (finance)!

While it is beyond the scope of this book to go into how to manage cash flow, create budgets, and record your accounts payable and receivable, I want to touch on just a few critical finance strategies that I see most business owners not implementing.

> Reading a business finance book is like trying to stay awake while my son tells me about his progress on Mine Craft. Very hard to do.

1. Invest in your Business.

If you are going into business to replace income from a job, please recognize that it frequently takes two years into a business before you pull a profit. Two years. Why would anyone want to work their butt off, work long hours without any guarantee of success, with no profit for two years? Because the payoff in the end can be fantastic, and the personal journey through the process is exhilarating.

> If you are going into business to replace income from a job, please recognize that it frequently takes two years into a business before you pull a profit.

If your expectation going into business is to pull a salary from your business as soon as you can, you will be limiting your company's survival rate dramatically. Unless you have funding, bootstrapping your business (building your business using business profits alone) will take every penny that the business brings in.

A good friend of mine did not invest as much as she needed to into her business, and it ended sadly.

Kaylee is a custom home builder. She quit her job working as a project manager for a larger home builder and decided to open her own business several years ago. After spending her savings and some credit card investments on some heavy efforts in marketing, she had a nice clientele base and after her first year was making more money than she had ever made before in her life. And this is when she made the mistake of not investing the profits back into her business.

Once she built up her clientele, she stopped her marketing efforts and paid herself a monthly salary that was more than she had ever made working as an employee. For six months she was living the dream! Then her client pool dried up and she was stuck. She hadn't invested the profits she made to attract the next wave of clients, choosing to pay herself instead. Her company was in trouble with no way to get more clients, and no cash or time to invest in marketing. Ouch!

One of the primary reasons small businesses never get off the ground is because they are underfunded. There simply isn't enough money to sustain the business. That was the case for Kaylee. Her options at that point were to seek out funding, whether from a loan or investors, or go back to the J-O-B. She chose to return to the world of employment.

How could she have played that scenario and still be in business? I would have encouraged her not to take income out at all if possible for as long as possible. If you aren't taking money out, you can invest that money into learning how to make your business profitable--your number one goal in the first year of your business.

After she had found a business strategy that worked and could pull a profit, the next year of business should have been spent in automating, systematizing, and scaling that business.

After that, she would be primed and ready to start paying herself nicely. At that point, her marketing would bring in a predictable number of leads which would turn into a predictable number of clients. She would have built a business machine that would pay out $5 for every $3 put in.

As weird as this might sound, I was so disappointed when I had to start paying myself from my business! In year two of my consulting business, I switched from an LLC into an S-Corp, which requires you to pay yourself as an employee with a salary that is consistent with the marketplace.

> I would have encouraged her not to take income out at all if possible for as long as possible. If you aren't taking money out, you can invest that money into learning how to make your business profitable - - your number one goal in the first year of business.

Instead of just taking money out when it made sense financially for the company, I now had to pay myself a regular salary. I was disappointed because I would always rather invest profit back into the company in the beginning, because I know it will produce income down the road that is much higher than the salary I take out.

2. Track Your Finances

Moving onto the second strategy that I strongly recommend, we need to talk about tracking your finances.

I know, I know. Telling you to track your finances is like telling you to exercise on a regular basis. Everyone knows it is good for them, but it is a hard thing to want to do.

One of the best ways to get yourself to do something that either intimidates you or is boring is to make yourself accountable to someone else, preferably someone you pay for.

It would be very worth your investment to hire a bookkeeper to sit down with you once a month for an hour. That would cost you $20 - $50, and would keep you organized and accountable to track your income and expenses.

If you aren't already tracking your finances on a monthly basis, put up an ad on Craigslist for a bookkeeper and get one to help you out!

I strongly recommend your using a service like QuickBooks or other accounting software. I like QuickBooks online because I can access it from any computer, which means that my bookkeeper and accountant can access it from their computers.

This one is easy to gloss over. If you aren't already working with a bookkeeper, add "put an ad on Craigslist for a bookkeeper" to your to-do list now. If you are waiting until you get your books in order to do it, that is like waiting for your house to get cleaned before you hire a housekeeper. There is no shame, whatever your books look like. Your bookkeeper exists to help you, not shame you.

3. Protect Yourself from Embezzlement

Now that you are investing your profits back into your business and tracking your finances, let's move on to the third strategy you must do. Protect yourself from embezzlement.

Embezzlement? Isn't that what happens in movies with guys dressed in black leather carrying bags of diamonds? No, it happens all of the time in small businesses with five or fewer employees. It happens in family businesses. Chances are good that it will happen to you or has already happened to you if you aren't employing the following guidelines. You just don't know about it.

Embezzling is the act of taking money that has been placed in your trust but belongs to another. As soon as you hire your first assistant that handles any finances, you have opened yourself up to the risk of embezzlement.

One of the best strategies to protect yourself from your employees siphoning money from the company for themselves is to divide up financial responsibilities.

One party should be in charge of writing checks and spending money. This will probably be you. You and only you will have access to the spending of money.

Another party is in charge of recording the transactions. This person takes your check stubs, credit card receipts and client payments, and records them all in QuickBooks.

A third party bookkeeper is in charge of checking the QuickBooks transactions against bank records and credit card statements that I supply for her each month. She catches anything that doesn't add up.

If you have three different people doing these duties (paying, recording, and balancing) you reduce the ability for any one of those people to embezzle from you. If you have one person doing any two of these tasks (unless that person is you), you are leaving yourself open to desperate employees taking advantage of the situation.

This list of three simple strategies is by no means inclusive of everything you need to know for financial health in your company. Here are some resources I recommend to help you with tracking your finances. A little bit of dread while you set these accounts up is guaranteed, but it is good for you!

1. Mint.com. This service is a free way to track your personal spending. Why is it on my list if it is personal finance tracking? A small business owner's business and personal finances are usually closely linked! I like to check this at night on my ipad before I go to bed.

2. Outright.com. This service is set up to be just like mint.com but for small business. I like to see all of my accounts at my fingertips. While it isn't how I track accounts receivable or taxes in my business, it is a good way to keep my business spending and budgets in mind. Track this weekly to keep spending habits in check!

3. Quickbooks online. I like using the Quickbooks online service so my virtual assistant and my bookkeeper can both login from their own locations. I also like that I don't have to worry about backing up my information--Quickbooks does that for me.

I love the quote, "There is nothing to fear except fear itself." This quote definitely applies to finances. Thinking about getting your finances in order is much more stressful than actually doing it. So do it.

Here are your action steps for this chapter:

1. Hire a bookkeeper if possible on your budget.

2. Track your finances on a spreadsheet if you are currently doing nothing.

3. Upgrade to Quickbooks if you are currently tracking on a spreadsheet.

CHAPTER 14

PLAYING BIG IN MARKETING

It was 2009. I was downstairs watching TV while my husband was putting the kids to bed. Flipping through the channels, I stopped at a commercial I was pretty sure was a skit on Saturday Night Live. When I realized it was a real infomercial, I immediately called my husband, "Mike! You have to come see this! It is HILARIOUS!"

The Infomercial was for the now well-known product, the Shake Weight. If you haven't seen it, you may not know the product's commercials have been described on MSNBC as being "slightly pornographic". Following its July 2009 debut, the Shake Weight infomercial went viral. Some YouTube parody clips about it have more than twelve million views.

Amid their success, fitness experts, doctors, and consumer advocates all say the same thing about the shake weight: you will get a much better workout doing regular dumbbell curls with a regular five pound dumbbell. It turns out the Shake Weight isn't a good product at all, but their marketing is fantastic. Shake Weight sales were up to $40M in 2010, and much higher than that three years later. You can make a lot of money with a really bad product as long as you have good marketing.

That is not to say that I am an advocate for creating really bad products. I think you have a moral responsibility as a small business owner to put good into the world. I am not going to be the product police; it is up to you to ensure you are in moral good standing with your product. I use this example just to illustrate that your company's success often has more to do with your marketing efforts than your product or service itself.

Let's dive deep into how to market a product.

What is marketing? Because the term is thrown around so loosely, people mean a lot of different things when they say marketing. Some people think it means branding, others think it means advertising or sales. The truth is it means all of those and more.

> My definition of marketing is: anything your business does to attract buying customers and invite them to make a purchase.

My definition of marketing is: anything your business does to attract buying customers and invite them to make a purchase.

There are so many options when it comes to marketing strategies that many small business owners get lost in the choices. I see entrepreneurs getting sucked into whatever looks new and sexy in marketing, instead of what their businesses actually need. This even happens with my own clients.

I host Internet Marketing Boot Camps several times a year for my high-end clients. I invite internet marketing experts from a variety of industries to present on their areas of expertise.

Several years ago I invited an expert on text marketing. Text marketing was new and exciting at the time, and the presenter was good-looking and funny. He charmed the crowd with his slick PowerPoint, and touted the wonders of text marketing with statistics showing how many people were using text to communicate, and how wonderful it would be to start marketing to those billions.

The problem is, text marketing is usually a good way to nurture existing clients but not to market to potential clients. I don't know about you, but I never want to receive unsolicited texts from any company, no matter how good the offer.

While at the Internet Marketing Boot Camp, my sweet client Abigail got excited about the possibility of using text marketing in her brand new business. She had no phone list to speak of, and had few existing clients that she could text. While she was in line to speak to Mr. Sexy Text Man, I had to intervene. I reminded her of the **SELLSUM** marketing system that she had previously learned from me (and I am about to teach you), showed her where text marketing fit within it, and suddenly she understood why text marketing was not a marketing strategy that she needed to spend her time and money implementing.

> The downside of using the SELLSUM system is it isn't very exciting and is decidedly unsexy, but the upside is no more wasted time and money on marketing techniques that you don't need.

If you take the time to review the **SELLSUM** marketing system that I am about to teach you before you make any marketing decision, you will stay focused on building a successful marketing funnel and prevent wasting time and money on marketing techniques that you just don't need.

You will never wonder again if you need to be on Twitter, Pinterest, Instagram, or LinkedIn. You will never question if you need to get a billboard, redesign your logo, or write a blog post. You will never try another flash-in-the pan marketing strategy because you will know that there is a very clear, very predictable 7-step sequence that you will build for every product you create. The **SELLSUM** marketing system takes the guesswork out of marketing.

Ready to revolutionize your marketing and take it from the spaghetti method (throwing spaghetti on the wall and seeing what sticks) into a systematized, predictable plan? The downside of using the **SELLSUM** system is it isn't very exciting and is decidedly unsexy, but the upside is no more wasted time and money on marketing techniques that you don't need.

Before we jump in to marketing, let's make this as simple as possible for you. You will need to determine your core product. What is the product that you sell again and again? If you are a retail store owner, your core product will be a category like shoes or lotions. If you have a product business and sell many products, choose your best-selling product, the one that you are most known for. If you are a service provider, choose the package or service that you sell most frequently. That is your core product.

Please don't move on until you have determined your core product.

Now that you have determined your core product, let's design a marketing plan for that core product. The first letter of the **SELLSUM** system is an S. The S of the **SELLSUM** system stands for STUFF.

This isn't stuff as in product stuff. It is stuff as in marketing stuff that you build that people can see.

STUFF: any marketing material that people can see

In the online world, STUFF would include your website, a webinar, blogs, videos, audios, commercials, ad copy, articles, social media platforms, etc.

In the off-line world (anything that isn't online) this would include fliers, billboards, brochures, business cards, presentation materials, banners, signs, and anything else that people can see.

Again, the STUFF is not your product. It is your marketing materials.

This is where we start. For every product you create, you need a STUFF. The purpose of the STUFF is to educate the buyer on your product. The first question you need to ask yourself is: Is your buyer most likely to find you online or offline? Meaning, will they find you while sitting in front of a computer, or anywhere except in front of a computer?

If they will find you primarily on a computer, you will choose an online STUFF. If they will find you somewhere else, you will choose an offline STUFF.

Let's give you an example of a product. If you design wedding dresses and determine that your core product is a dress and your typical client will find you online, your first step would be to create a website with your dresses featured on it. Done. Check. You don't have to create ALL of the STUFF examples, you just start with one.

Now think of YOUR core product, and the customer buying it. Are they going to find you online or offline? What is the first STUFF that you will need to create?

Go ahead and take a blank sheet of paper, and write your core product name on the top. Write the letters **SELLSUM** running down the left hand side of your paper. Now choose just one STUFF and put it next to the S.

I'll show you an example of a service business: Sue has a financial training business, and her core product is a $197 live workshop. She would write that on the top of the page. Then for S, she would choose just one STUFF that she is currently using, or would like to use. She could choose "website" as her online STUFF. If she is marketing offline, she could choose "expo booth" as her STUFF.

You will probably have multiple STUFF's currently in your business, but you will not write all of them down. You will only write one. This is important! We will follow only one sequence. If you list a bunch of STUFF's, you will not be able to see the relationship between the STUFF and the next step. Choose only ONE STUFF.

Eventually, you will build out **SELLSUM** funnels for every product and for multiple STUFFs, but for now you will just write one.

Let's talk about the common mistakes in the STUFF category.

Small business owners often fall into the trap of spending a lot of their time creating and purchasing STUFF. They might have an awesome website, stacks of brochures everywhere, beautiful signage, a library of marketing videos on YouTube, but if they aren't investing time and money on step number two, all of those marketing dollars are wasted. You must go through the entire **SELLSUM** system for each product.

Step number two in the **SELLSUM** system is E for EYEBALLS. Are there eyeballs looking at your stuff? When I ask that question to a small business owner, they will usually tell me, "Yes, people see my website. And I post on Facebook." Let's not think in terms of vague generalities. Nope, I want a systematized, predictable way for you to get EYEBALLS on your STUFF.

EYEBALLS: what you do to get eyeballs looking at your STUFF

Here are some examples:

Online:
- Google ads
- Facebook ads
- YouTube ads
- Banner ads
- Affiliate email marketing
- Joint webinars or telesummits
- Buying email or phone lists or renting lists, etc.

Offline:
- Renting billboard space
- Sending out Mailers
- Radio spots
- Cold-calling
- Door-knocking
- Cross promotions with affiliate partners
- Attending expos and trade shows
- Attending networking events, etc.

These aren't presented as all-inclusive checklists that you run your finger down while saying, "Do it, want to try it, wouldn't work in my industry." Less important than understanding what each of these methods looks like is understanding what the category of EYEBALLS does. It gets a predictable number of people to view your STUFF.

As you can see from these sample lists, getting eyeballs on your stuff requires concerted effort, time, and usually money on your part. This isn't just posting a few links on your Facebook page, or sending out an email blast to your existing list. Promoting your products to your existing list of eyeballs is important and always included in any marketing effort, but you must also go outside of your current network and start getting new, fresh eyeballs to look at your STUFF.

You already chose your STUFF for your core product. If it is an online STUFF, you will now choose one online EYEBALLS method to drive traffic to that STUFF. Just one. If it is an offline STUFF, you will now choose an offline EYEBALLS method.

For example, in Sue's financial training business with a core product as a $197 live training, she chose a website as the STUFF, and she can now choose Facebook Ads as her eyeballs.

It would look like this on her paper:

Core product: $197 Live Financial Training

S: Website
E: Facebook Ad

If she chose to do an offline marketing funnel it would look like this:

Core product: $197 Live Financial Training

S: Expo booth (tablecloth, banner, flyers)
E: Expo

In the example above, the expo drives traffic for her, so she doesn't need to do anything more for EYEBALLS.

After you have mastered that one EYEBALLS method and you know it works for your business, and you have an actual number indicating how many views or clicks or people saw it, you are ready to move on to adding an additional EYEBALLS method to drive even more traffic. But we are going to start with just one. Yes, even if you are awesome. Just one.

If all of the EYEBALLS methods are unknown or scary for you, but you are

> We are going to start with just one. Yes, even if you awesome. Just one.

serious about growing your business and becoming a real business owner instead of a hobbyist, I invite you to join me for a year-long business training and coaching program that will change your life. Your first step would be to attend a Business Intensive Retreat. Yep, that is my core product.

Now that you are driving traffic or EYEBALLS to your STUFF, your next step in the SELLSUM is LEAD COLLECTION. LEAD COLLECTION is especially important if you are selling a higher-end product (anything above $149) but it is important for any business.

What is a LEAD? A lead is a potential client name with the information your company would need to contact him. For example, a name, a phone number, and an email or mailing address. If you go to a networking group and talk to five people who are interested in purchasing your widget, and you collected their business cards, you now have five leads.

LEAD COLLECTION: getting names and contact information from people who are interested in your product

But what if you sell a lower-end product, you ask? I worked with a client years ago who sold photo calendars online. Her average calendar was $39, and her clients found her online and purchased online. She didn't understand why she needed to collect leads if the buyer simply went to her website and either decided they liked the calendar or didn't like it, purchased it or didn't purchase it, and moved on.

The reason she should be collecting leads as well as selling is this: she is limiting her buying pool to only those who were ready to purchase the second they find her site. They either are in the perfect buying space the second they see her site, or they are gone forever.

What if her potential client found her site, was interested, then realized she needed to pick up her child from school? Or couldn't find her credit card? Or wanted to check with her daughter first before purchasing? Or thought the calendar would be a great gift for Christmas, 5 months away? Or wasn't sure yet if it would be the perfect wedding gift? Or wanted to do some more research about your company?

There are a million reasons why prospective buyers who find you the first time don't purchase from you the first time they see you. They often need more time, and more "touches" with your company to be comfortable purchasing.

When my calendar client realized this, she added an opt-in form to her website. To get them to opt-in, she added a simple freebie downloadable calendar with her branding on it that clients could use to record their family birthdays. She started collecting leads and growing her list.

A client lead is a valuable thing! In your business, leads could be worth $1 each, or could be worth $100 each. We are happy to "pay" for that lead on our website by offering something of value in exchange for someone's information.

After my calendar client had the leads, she could continue to market to them and take them through the complete **SELLSUM** System. Without those leads, she was leaving dollars behind as she was only working with instant buyers.

Let's think about our wedding dress designer example again. She could drive thousands of EYEBALLS to her STUFF, but if she simply asked them to purchase a wedding dress directly from her website, she might not sell many dresses. She needs to take them to the next step of the **SELLSUM** system.

Leads are usually collected online through an opt-in form or registration form, on a social media platform by "liking" or "following" your business, and offline through a business card, or a registration or sign-up form.

Let's go back to Sue's financial training business. Here is what she has on her page on her online funnel:

Core product: $197 Live Financial Training

S: Website
E: Facebook Ad
L: Opt-in form on website to get a free debt analysis quiz

Here is what she has on her page as an offline funnel:

Core product: $197 Live Financial Training

S: Expo booth (tablecloth, banner, flyers)
E: Expo
L: Registration forms to win a free financial organization kit

On the **SELLSUM** page that you are creating, go ahead and write down what your LEAD COLLECTION method will be. At this point, you will not create both an offline and an online funnel. Just create one for now. How are you going to collect LEADS?

The next step of the **SELLSUM** system is LEAD NURTURE. A client of mine named Melanie learned the importance of LEAD NURTURE the hard way.

Melanie went to her first expo and set up a beautiful booth. Her STUFF included a banner, a nice table display with her product, and flyers for her bridal floral design business. She had EYEBALLS through the expo itself, and she was doing LEAD COLLECTION through a drawing for a bridal bouquet. She followed the SELLSUM system perfectly up to this point.

When the expo ended, she immediately jumped on the phone and called all 100 leads that she got and asked them if they wanted to purchase a bridal bouquet. Unfortunately, hours on the phone only awarded her one client, and she was understandably discouraged.

Melanie realized that she had forgotten the next step of the **SELLSUM**. She had forgotten the LEAD NURTURE step. Many of the leads she called didn't know who she was, didn't even remember signing up for her drawing because there were so many booths at the expo, and didn't feel comfortable buying from her yet.

LEAD NURTURE: building your relationship with your leads through free stuff or experiences with you

LEAD NURTURE is most easily done through email. Whether you get your leads from an online opt-in form, or from an off-line piece of paper, the first thing you do with those leads is enter them into your ESP (Email Service Provider) like Mailchimp, Constant Contact, Aweber, or InfusionSoft.

To follow spam laws, you must ask people if they would like to get regular emails from you. In an online opt-in form, they give you permission when they enter their name and information. In an off-line drawing or registration form, you can either have a check-box that says, "Yes! I would like to get a free xyz" so they can opt-in to your

> Instead of bragging about you, focus on educating them on your industry.

email list, or you could email them a single email saying something like, "It was so good to meet you at xyz expo! I would love to give you a free xyz. Please click the link to get this free gift. " Then you would link to an opt-in form on your website.

You will nurture your leads by sending them relevant information and education about your industry. Sharing articles or videos with your leads about how great your company is, or what sets it apart from your competitors, does not qualify as relevant information about your industry.

Instead of bragging about you, focus on educating them on your industry. For example, in Sue's financial training company she could send twice-monthly emails with three-minute videos on the following topics:

- How to balance your checkbook
- The number one indicator that you will go bankrupt
- The best plan to pay off credit cards
- How to track your spending in 5 minutes a week

In the wedding dress design business, the owner could send monthly email articles about the following topics:

- How to style your hair to match the style of your dress
- What your dress says about your personality
- The top 10 most popular dress styles this year
- 3 Biggest catering mistakes and how to avoid them

Notice that she hasn't sent an article on why her dresses are better than her competitors'. Instead of bragging, the goal is to build a relationship with your leads (or "list") and show them that you are an expert in your industry.

Let's add this step to Sue's financial training example. Here is her online funnel:

Core product: $197 Live Financial Training

S: Website
E: Facebook Ad
L: Opt-in form on website to get a free debt analysis quiz
L: Free training videos every other week

Here is what she has on her page as an offline funnel:

Core product: $197 Live Financial Training

S: Expo booth (tablecloth, banner, flyers)
E: Expo
L: Registration forms to win a free financial organization kit
L: Email inviting them to get the free training videos

Now it is your turn to record your LEAD NURTURE on your **SELLSUM** page. If using an ESP (Email Service Provider) is new for you, know that this is an important step in growing your business. Don't use the excuse of "I don't have a big list so I don't need one." You build your list on an ESP! That excuse is like saying, "I'll buy a refrigerator when I get cold food." It doesn't make any sense.

To read my reviews on different Email Service Providers, please visit my Kim Recommends page on my website: kimflynn.com

We are done with four steps of the **SELLSUM** system already. We have built websites, created and paid for ads, spent hours at expo booths and networking groups, and spent months building an autoresponder sequence with our ESP. At this point, we have invested quite a bit of time and money, but notice that we haven't made a dime. We don't make any sales until the next step, the SALES. You will need to ask for the sale.

SALE: the point when you ask a prospective customer (lead) if they want to purchase. Your company will ask all leads for the sale after they have been nurtured. Yep, all leads.

No one needed to implement the SALES step in their marketing more than my friend Elizabeth. Elizabeth was a well-known life coach who hosted events, wrote books, and spoke on stages, but she had never been able to make more than a couple thousand dollars a year. She was known to the media, had regular TV appearances and wrote a regular article in a local magazine. She had mastered all of the steps in the **SELLSUM** until she got to S. She never asked for the sale.

I attended one of her large women's events. She had STUFF: she had beautifully designed banners, event programs, and a stack of flyers on the table about her programs. There were table displays on each table outlining her programs.

She had EYEBALLS. She had media appearances, email blasts, social media campaigns, and even a flyer blitz to local boutiques and shops. Over 100 women came to the event.

She had LEAD COLLECTION. Everyone registered online, and she dutifully collected names, emails and phone numbers.

She had LEAD NURTURE. Her speakers were all well-known, and gave beautiful presentations on topics that were interesting. Her own presentation was well-crafted and useful to the audience. She had coaches doing free one-on-one coaching sessions.

And, she never asked for a sale. She never mentioned the specifics of her offer from stage. She didn't train her coaches to tell the women about the products she offered. The only way a woman in attendance would have known about her offer was if she read the fine print on a flyer.

In the group of over 100, only three people purchased the $197 coaching kit. She lost thousands of dollars on the event. She did all the work, took 100 people down the first four steps of the SELLSUM System--the hard part--and stopped right before she could have been profitable. Tragic!

Think about your current marketing. Every lead that comes in your email, every person who follows you on Facebook, every business card you collect, and every person that enters your drawings will eventually have the sales conversation. Every person.

The SALES conversation might be an actual phone conversation for a high-end product, might be a lunch meeting or an event for a very high-end product, might be on a webinar presentation or a sales page, or might even be an offer directly in email. Every lead needs to be brought to the SALES conversation. We do not wait for her to ask for the sales conversation. We determine ahead of time how long the nurture phase is, and at what point we ask for the sale. After she has gone through the nurture phase, we have the conversation.

Let's go back to our Financial Training example:

Core product: $197 Live Financial Training

S: Website
E: Facebook Ad
L: Opt-in form on website to get a free debt analysis quiz
L: Free training videos every other week
S: Call leads 7 days after opt-in

Here is what she has on her page as an offline funnel:

Core product: $197 Live Financial Training

S: Expo booth (tablecloth, banner, flyers)
E: Expo
L: Registration forms to win a free financial organization kit
L: Email inviting them to get the free training videos
S: Call leads 3 days after event

In this example, all leads get a phone call on a pre-determined date after they are nurtured. The online funnel and the offline funnel converge.

I work with many clients who do network marketing. One of the biggest problems I see for them is the date to have the sales conversation is often not set. Network marketers say things like, "Well, I like to give them lots of samples. And when I feel they are ready, I ask for the sale."

I challenge you to take all feelings out of marketing! Going with your gut may work well when you have five leads, but I want you to get to the point of getting fifty leads per week. You can't go with your gut on fifty; you will lose track and most will slip between the cracks. Most slip between the cracks even with five leads!

Instead, you are going to build a system. A beautiful, predictable system in which a lead will enter the system, and just like clockwork, will be nurtured with an email series, then called seven or two or ten days later. To grow your business, you will need to embrace systems.

Let's do an example of a low-end $10 product:
Core product: $10 Eczema Lotion

S: Sales page
E: Google Ads
L: Pop up on page that offers coupon emailed to them
L: Monthly emails on eczema topics
S: Offer in each monthly email

In a low-end product, there will be many buyers who will be nurtured enough on the sales page itself that they will buy on the spot. That is our low-hanging fruit, and we definitely want to get those immediate sales. If you offer a coupon mailed to them or another enticing offer as well as the immediate sale, you will also grow your email list beyond those people who are ready to buy this second.

One of my clients has an online dress store, and she has used this method to grow her list to 75,000 over the past five years. When you have your own list of 75,000 you can simply send out an email with an offer and make thousands of dollars.

How are you going to ask for the SALE? Please record this on your own **SELLSUM** page.

The next two steps of the **SELLSUM** are not to be even considered until you master the first five steps.

The U stands for UPSERVE. How can you serve your client or customer to an even higher level than your core product?

UPSERVE or UPSELL: a higher-end product with a higher price point

My core product is a Business Intensive Retreat. At the retreats, my clients learn and implement the **SELLSUM** Marketing System, as well as the Plug & Play Business System to run their companies. They come away with clarity on exactly what they need to do to grow their businesses, as well as a step-by-step system to follow every day to run their businesses.

But if all I offered was a Business Intensive Retreat, I wouldn't be serving my client to my capacity. Many clients want more than a three-day Intensive. Many clients want to go through an entire year learning how to run all areas of their business: their leadership, marketing, product development, client fulfillment, and finance. They can't learn everything they need to know in three days.

> You will need to understand that your business is more important than the product your business sells. Your business is the product. Your product isn't the business.

To upserve my client who wants more, my company also offers year-long business training programs. We call these high-end clients teamELITE.

If I didn't offer teamELITE programs, I would not be serving my clients to my potential. Many would leave the retreats wanting more, and would be frustrated that they couldn't find an all-inclusive business training program. If I didn't offer teamELITE programs, my business would also be missing out on a lot of revenue.

Think about your own business. Do you have a high-end UPSERVE? This program or product might not be for every client, but there will be some who are needing your high-end product.

Let's show you some examples. Here is a sample Upserve for the Financial Training company:

Core product: $197 Live Financial Training

S: Expo booth (tablecloth, banner, flyers)
E: Expo

L: Registration forms to win a free financial organization kit
L: Email inviting them to get the free training videos
S: Call leads
U: Priority seating at the event

Here is an Upserve idea for the Eczema Lotion company:

Core product: $10 Eczema Lotion

S: Sales page
E: Google Ads
L: Pop up on page that offers coupon emailed to them
L: Monthly emails on eczema topics
S: Offer in each monthly email
U: Lotion packs with all 10 varieties

What can you do to UPSERVE your client? Record that now on your **SELLSUM** page.

We are on the last step of the **SELLSUM** system! This last step requires that you fully understand a concept that we mentioned earlier in this book. You will need to understand that your business is more important than the product your business sells. Your business is the product. Your product isn't the business.

As you go through the **SELLSUM** steps, you will collect a large number of people in your email list. You will have a social media following. You will be recognized as an expert in your industry. If you are a financial trainer, you will have collected a large list of people who are interested in financial principles, probably women in their 40's who have families. If you are a wedding dress designer, you will have collected an email list of soon-to-be newlyweds who are primarily women in their 20's.

If you have the limiting mindset that your product is your business, you won't be able to do anything more with that list of 40-year old women than sell them your financial training. For those people who don't buy your financial training, you will have nothing more to offer them, and all the money and time you spent collecting that list will be useless. You have a resource (your list) and you aren't using that resource to its fullest.

If you have a more expansive business mindset, and understand that your entire business is the product, you will want to utilize every resource in your business. That list is a resource for so much more than just selling your own financial training or selling your own wedding dresses.

It is time to ask yourself, what else does this person need? What more could a 40-year old mother need? What other products could a 25-year old newlywed need?

The answer is a lot! You will reach out to reputable companies who are looking for this same target market. Twenty something new brides might purchase products for their new homes, trendy clothing and shoes, inexpensive vacations, and skin care products. You could reach out to other women in business who have products and services like these and ask them if they would like to be an affiliate partner.

The last step of the **SELLSUM** system is MERGE AFFILIATE OFFERS. You can't possibly make a product for every need that your target market has, but you should be utilizing the list you have built to make money on affiliate offers.

MERGE AFFILIATE OFFERS: offering other companies' products to your list, and getting a referral fee, or affiliate commission, from each purchase

Whenever I send people to my Kim Recommends page on KimFlynn.com, I am inviting them to purchase from an affiliate of mine. These are business products and services that my company doesn't provide (like web design, web hosting, graphic design, etc) that my clients regularly purchase. Knowing that they will need to find companies to provide these services, I share these hand-picked reputable companies to recommend to my clients, and I get a referral, or affiliate, fee for every client who purchases through my link.

What products or services do your clients also purchase? Record that on your **SELLSUM** page. Here is the financial trainer example:

S: Expo booth (tablecloth, banner, flyers)
E: Expo

L: Registration forms to win a free financial organization kit
L: Email inviting them to get the free training videos
S: Call leads
U: Priority seating at the event
M: Bill-paying kit

Here is the Eczema Lotion company:

Core product: $10 Eczema Lotion

S: Sales page
E: Google Ads
L: Pop up on page that offers coupon emailed to them
L: Monthly emails on eczema topics
S: Offer in each monthly email
U: Lotion packs with all 10 varieties
M: Natural mineral make-up

After you add the last step, you have completed your **SELLSUM** Marketing System! Whenever I teach this presentation live, I always take a hand raise poll on which piece of the **SELLSUM** business owners are missing. Without fail, the most neglected pieces of the SELLSUM are EYEBALLS, LEAD NURTURE, and asking for the SALE.

Once you have mastered one funnel, and you have a predictable number of eyeballs leading to a predictable number of leads leading to a predictable number of sales, you are ready to take the next step towards business growth.

Here are the growth choices for a business owner. Let's use Sue's financial advising company as our example. I want you to pretend you are a business advisor for just a minute, and you will tell Sue which growth method she should choose next.

Once Sue has her core product, her $197 financial training seminars, with a consistent, predictable, systematized **SELLSUM** funnel, she is ready for the next step. Should she:

A. Create a new product?
She could decide she wants to have not only a one-day event for $197, but she also wants an online event for $49/month.

B. Do more of the same EYEBALLS method that already works?

She gets 100 leads on average for each expo, which brings in 10 people for each event. Expos are predictable and systematized. To grow more with EYEBALLS, she signs up for even more expo events.

C. Add a different EYEBALLS method?

She has heard good things about Facebook ads, and wants to start running ads targeting her local customer.

> We are going to set passion aside for a while, and actually make money first. Life coaches across the world are hating me for saying that, but I want your business to survive!

What would you advise Sue to do first?

The most common answer when women run their business without a system is to create a new product. *Sigh* Please don't do that. Product creation is fun and exciting and creative and gets your passion juices flowing, but it also is expensive, time-consuming, and doesn't bring in income. We are going to set passion aside for a while, and actually make money first. Life coaches across the world are hating me right now for saying that, but I want your business to survive!

The smartest way to grow your business is simply to put more money and time into choice B. If you have built a system that requires you to put $1 in to get $3 out, you have built a powerful machine. If you put $100 into it and you get $300 out, you have just made $200 profit.

If you have built this machine, why would you ever choose to invest money building another machine, when you have one you haven't capitalized on yet? Now, instead of putting $100 into the machine, put in $1000. You will get $3000 out.

Once you have money coming in from your first path to profitability (selling product in a consistent method using the **SELLSUM** system) you are ready to move on to choice C in the growth choices. You will need to try different methods of getting EYEBALLS.

This is why you will need to experiment with different marketing methods: when I started my consulting business in 2009, affiliate email marketing was hot. I could ask affiliates to send out an email to their lists, inviting their lists to my teleseminar. Their lists would respond, and I would get many opt-ins to my list.

Affiliate emailing was the foundation of my marketing, and we brought in 80% of our clientele through this method. Unfortunately, now I get very low responses to affiliate email marketing. If I used to get 25 opt-ins from every affiliate. My average before I killed my company's email affiliate program altogether was three. Three leads per affiliate. That isn't worth my company's time or effort. If I had continued to run this model without looking for alternative EYEBALLS methods, my company would not be alive today.

Each marketing method seems to have a shelf life. Trends come and go, and if you rely on one and only one marketing method, when that method no longer works your company will have to scramble to find a new method, test it, tweak it, and then start running it. If the find, test, tweak process takes you six months, you would have six months of little revenue coming in.

Rather than scramble once you realize your marketing method is no longer working, plan for that marketing method no longer working. As soon as you have your first SELLSUM system running predictably, and you are pouring money into it, start testing other methods. As soon as you have your second marketing system running predictably, then do choice B, and pour more money into system number two. Then start testing system number three.

I have business owners ask me all of the time, "How do you get your leads?" and I have to laugh. We do almost everything under the sun. We host webinars, live events, do online summits, strategic social media, do expos and trade shows, speak all over the country, write articles, film videos, do Facebook and Google Ads, run YouTube video ads, sponsor charity events, and pay a PR company to name a few. But I started out with just one method, and I suggest you do too.

Here are your action steps for this chapter:

- Write out a SELLSUM system for your core product

- Begin creating your system, starting with the S

CHAPTER 15

THE DAY WHEN

One day, when you have struggled long enough to figure out how to market your product, how to lead your team, how to produce a product that has a demand, how to serve your customer beautifully, and you have money flowing in, it will hit you: Oh my goodness, I have actually MADE IT.

I remember that day clearly for me. My sales team had just closed $185,000 in one day. After years spent dreaming of "the day when", and working towards "the day when", that day had finally arrived.

After reaching "the day when", I realized that I had put some expectations on money that money can never fulfill. To explain that, I first have to tell you a story about me and exercise.

About ten years ago I went on an extreme diet and exercise program. It was a popular program at the time, and all marketing efforts showed pictures of an overweight before picture followed not just by a thin-after picture, but a completely buff after-picture. I was hooked.

There was one before picture in the exercise program of a woman who had a build similar to mine. Her before picture was a healthy size eight with some roll on the tummy and lack of toning in the thighs. I could relate. Her after picture was amazing; her legs were not just slim but they were sculpted and her abs were defined. She was the epitome of my dream body.

I followed that diet and exercise twelve-week program to the letter. I ate little more than chicken and whole wheat bread for three months. I worked out six days a week with weights and cardio. I pushed myself to my limit almost every day. I constantly thought of the woman's picture with the perfect abs and shaped legs. And I slowly developed her figure.

After twelve weeks I had lost almost twenty pounds. I went to the tanning salon, put on a bikini, and posed while flexing for my own after pictures. When I saw them on my computer monitor I was shocked. I looked just like my ideal. I looked fantastic. And I felt cheated.

> Unfortunately, creating an ideal body didn't change anything about me except my body. I was looking for something more significant and didn't find it in exercise.

Somewhere in my mind was the idea that if I had the perfect body, my life would instantly transform. I would be super confident, would always feel great about myself, would be uber-Kim instead of regular old Kim. Uber-Kim was amazingly happy, filled with energy and joy every day at just the prospect of life. She never ignored her kids and felt guilty about it; she never let the house go; she never snapped at her husband; she never struggled with feelings of inadequacy. Uber-Kim was amazing.

Unfortunately, creating an ideal body didn't change anything about me except my body. I was looking for something more significant and didn't find it in exercise.

On "the day when" in my business I felt a similar feeling. "You mean, this is it? Money doesn't change anything fundamental about who I am? I still have bad days? I still have days when I doubt myself? I still feel inadequate at times? And I still feel pressure to do more?" I realized I had been chasing money for the same reason I had been chasing the perfect body; I was looking for the uber-life instead of just regular life, with money.

When you have money flowing into your business, your problems will not go away. Making money is not the answer to your prayers. Making money is simply making money.

What is money, anyway?

My favorite definition of money is: the power to do.

It took me about a week after "the day when" to get my bearings and realize that money in itself wasn't a worthy goal to chase. What IS a worthy goal to chase is the power to do.

I have a strong desire to lead women. I lead women to trust themselves, to fulfill their potential, and connect to God. That is what I do, and business is the vehicle I am using to do that.

When I make money in my business, I have even more power to do what I want to do: touch and inspire even more women to trust themselves, fulfill their potential, and connect to God.

The purpose of business is to make money, and the purpose of money is to DO.

> My favorite definition of money is: the power to do.

With this definition in mind, now I can never get enough money! I want as much power to do big things as I can get. I want to help and influence women, and leave the world a better place.

Sometimes I hear people fantasize about what they will do after "the day when." I hear them talk about traveling the world, retiring on an island, and never working again. If you are the kind of person who took the time, had the persistence and used your talent to actually make it to "the day when," chances are you won't want to retire; you will work again; and you will probably work a lot again. Retiring on an island might be the very last choice you would ever make.

My husband and I go on a Caribbean vacation every year. Several years ago we went to the Cayman Islands and visited what is called Stingray City. A tour boat took us out to what seemed like the middle of the ocean, where a giant sand berg lies just a few feet under the water. After years of tourist visits, stingrays now congregate there knowing the tourists will feed them. The stingrays have become tame, and you can hand feed them.

Getting out of the tour boat in Stingray city, I noticed a couple on a small yacht sitting fifty feet away. They were very tan, and with drinks in their hands they called out to us in American English. "Hey, do you want to come party with us? This is our boat!"

I was so heartbroken for this couple. If they were bored enough to come out to Stingray City to find tourists to hang out with, they were fairly desperate for some meaning in their lives. They had made it to "the day when," and instead of doing something useful with their money and exercising their power to do, they had bought into believing that non-activity and a nice boat would be their ticket into the uber-life. Instead, they were still living normal life, just on a boat, bored out of their minds, and slightly drunk.

What if, instead of buying a yacht and moving to an island, they had agreed to vacation there whenever they needed a break, and spend the rest of their time and money DOING? What if they taught children in their area how to read, or mentored teenage runaways, or gathered donations to educate children in Guatemala, or started an orphanage in Uganda? When you have the power to do, you move into another phase of your life. Instead of being on the receiving end, you are now on the giving end. You can extend opportunities instead of just taking them.

> The purpose of business is to make money, and the purpose of money is to DO.

I believe we were put on earth to create! The talents we were born with, plus the time and effort we spend developing our skills are our raw tools. It is up to us to step persistently, day after day, even when it isn't sexy or exciting, in the direction of growth and creation.

That is what I call playing BIG in business.

Here are your action steps for this chapter:

1. Brainstorm a list of things that you want to do with your power to do. This is a great use for a Vision Board!

2. Consider coming to a Business Intensive Retreat if you haven't already registered: www.womensbusinessretreat.com I would love to see you there!

GLOSSARY OF TERMS

These are not dictionary definitions. These are my definitions of business jargon, as I use them in this book. I have tried to make these definitions reader friendly and the opposite of legal-eze, so please consult your attorney or tax accountant for complete definitions if desired.

Accounts Payable: This is an account you use to record how much money your business owes to others

Accrual basis: A way of tracking your business finances that takes into account when people purchase now but pay later, and when you purchase now and pay later. You get more accurate finance numbers when you use accrual basis instead of cash basis.

Accounts Receivable: This is an account you use to record how much money your customers owe you. If you allow your clients to purchase now but pay later or pay in increments, you will list the money owed to you in your Accounts Receivable.

Asset: Something you have ownership of. This might be a building, intellectual property, or cash in the bank.

Autoresponder: A series of emails that you set up in your ESP (email service provider) that sends out automatically when a client enters their information into your opt-in form, for example

Balance Sheet: A list that shows a snapshot of your company's financial information. It will list your assets, your liabilities, and your equity.

Bootstrapping: Growing your business using only your own funds. This includes money the company makes, personal funds, and personal credit cards.

Cash basis: A way of tracking your business finances that ignores money owed to you, or money you owe. It simply tracks how much cash you have spent and received.

Cash flow: The status of your business having cash or not having cash. For example, if you have $100,000 in an accounts receivable account (owed to you), but no cash coming in, your business may be highly profitable, but you have no cash flow.

Conversion ratio: How many people purchase your product compared to how many people you talk to. For example, if you talk to 10 people about buying your gizmo, and 2 people purchase, you have a 20% conversion.

Copy: The written part of any marketing piece. As in, "John, have you finished writing that ad copy yet?"

Core product: The primary product your business sells

CPA: Certified Public Accountant

Cross-sell: After the customer has purchased a product, you can offer another product in the same price range.

Double entry accounting: Each activity is entered into your accounting software, like Quickbooks, with both an item and an account it came from. For example, if you made a $100 sale, you would make two entries: you would add $100 to an account called "Cash" and add the same amount to an account called "Income". The purpose of double entry accounting is to allow you to track your income by accrual instead of just cash basis.

Downline: In an MLM, or multi-level marketing business, the people that sign up underneath you as distributors are called your downline

Downsell: After the customer has refused an offer, you offer a downsell. This is a less expensive offer.

ESP: (email service provider). The popular ones include Mailchimp, Aweber, Constant Contact, iContact, and Infusionsoft. ESP's are very useful to collect your lead list. You will generally want to email your entire list at least once a month.

Equity: Your claim in your company. Just as a bank would have a claim on a $10,000 loan you borrowed, you also have a claim on some of your cash. If you have $15,000 in the bank (your assets) and you subtracted the $10,000 claim from the bank (your liability), the remainder would be $5000, or your equity. You determine owner's equity by subtracting assets - liabilities.

Fulfillment: Working with your client to fulfill on your contract or obligation with them. For example, if you are a piano teacher, teaching the piano lessons is the fulfillment portion of your business. You generally want to hire out all or most of fulfillment.

Liabilities: The claim that others have on your assets. For example, if you have a bank loan for $10,000, you would list that in your liabilities. The $10,000 cash would then be listed in your assets list.

List: When I say list, I am talking about your email list. You house your list on an ESP (email service provider) like Mailchimp, Aweber, Constant Contact, or Infusionsoft.

LLC: Limited Liability Corporation. An LLC protects you from lawsuits against the company going after your personal assets. You file taxes for an LLC with your personal taxes, which makes it easier than an S-Corp.

Marketing: Anything your business does to communicate with prospective clients with the goal of selling product

MLM: Multi-level Marketing Business, or a network marketing business. These businesses are a great way to go if you are a natural connector, and if you don't want to create your own product.

Online product: A product that is consumed online. These are usually training courses, videos, audios, etc.

Optimize: Usually used along with the word SEO. To SEO optimize your website (or optimize a blog post) you would ensure the coding is ideal for Google to read the content, and find what keywords are important in that content.

Opt-in: When someone goes to your website and enters their name and contact information, the do that on an opt-in form. They have then opted in!

Profit: How much revenue your company made minus your expenses. For example, if you sold a $100 purse in your store, and you spent $30 to purchase that purse, your profit is $70

Residual Income: A pet peeve phrase of Kim's. This is touted heavily in the MLM industry. It does mean you will make additional earnings off of your downline's sales. It rarely means you will be able to sit back and do nothing while your team makes millions of dollars for you for the rest of your life.

Revenue: money your business makes. Gross income.

ROI: Return on investment. If you spend $10 on an ad and make $100 in sales your ROI is better than if you spend $10 on an ad and make $50 in sales.

S-Corp: A corporation that files its taxes separately from the owner's taxes. When you have an S-Corp you will generally pay less taxes as an owner. S-Corps require you to pay yourself a salary.

SEO: Search Engine Optimization. The art of getting your website to the top of the search engines in Google. While this was an effective strategy in the past, changes that Google made to their algorithms now makes paying for SEO a much more expensive and long-term marketing strategy than it used to be.

Sole Proprietorship: This is the most basic form of a business. You simply register with your state that you are doing business. You can file your business name as yourself, or under a DBA (doing business as). Sole Proprietorships don't protect your personal assets if your company were to be sued.

Upsell: I also call this upserve. Once a customer purchases one item, you ask them to purchase another item. The upsell offer is usually, but doesn't have to be, more expensive than the first.

VA: Virtual Assistant. This is an assistant who does work for you online. He/she can live in your town, or across the world.

Vision Board: A poster board with pictures of things that inspire you. This is a great way to get motivated in your life. It is not a good way to build a business.

ACKNOWLEDGMENTS

I would love to acknowledge editing and formatting help, needed encouragement, and honest feedback from the lovely Tiffany Berg Coughran. Thank you so much for killing my first version of a book; that needed to happen. True friends always tell the truth, and you are a true friend.

I also want to acknowledge my children. Beautiful Brenley, inside and out. Jason the focused, who is fearless. Austin, who is walking joy. Bria, who is a handful of perfection.

Thank you to my clients, past and present, whose experiences are referenced throughout this book. You continue to inspire me every time you stumble, get discouraged, and get right back in the saddle. You have influenced my life deeply. I love ya'll.

An extra shout out goes to a few of my teamELITIST clients: fabulous Lisa Rehurek, may you drive that backhoe one day; natural born leader Emili Whitney, the master room commandeer; the uber-talented, creatively competent Heidi Totten; the sales master Amy Walker who dreams of being a hippie; the very funny Teddy Hodges and his ahem, silk underwear; the bold and brassy Michelle Smith, who asked me if I grew up in a barn; Plug & Play master Erin Mathie who schools me in the art of spreadsheets; and one of the kindest people I know, Melissa Bamfo, who serenaded us in the hot tub with her hair blowing in the wind. I am so honored to call you friends.

A special acknowledgement goes out to my team who runs Kim Flynn Consulting efficiently and with care. Thank you especially to our long-term MVP Wendy Hinckley, Karen Heap who works magic with the books, assistant extraordinaire Lindsey Burton, Lindsay Fairbanks who takes care of our clients, Erica Persson and Lizzy Sanft who work hard to host our events, Heather Nitta who is my handler (among many other titles), and my very talented sales team lead by the lovely Chelsey Mowen. I am so thankful for you.

Thank you also to my core team of trainers and coaches. The lovely Jon Rogers (Mr. Over-compensation himself, too soon?, and the most brilliant business mind I know), Rebekah Hall (the best coach to ever swim in the deep end without floaties, I'm glad you belong to my community), and my Aunt Lisa Smith (my original inspiration to be a trainer, hoping this book inspires another 12 year old like your book did for me). I appreciate you all more than you know.

ABOUT THE AUTHOR

Kim Flynn is a highly sought-after speaker for women in business and the creator of the Plug & Play Business System. After three years as a school teacher, Kim started her first tutoring business when she was 24 years old. She grew that business to employ over 30 people, and then sold that business and two others in 2010 when she founded Kim Flynn Consulting. Kim is passionate about helping entrepreneurs, and has made it her mission to inspire women (and a few brave men) to play BIG in business. She leads monthly retreats to train entrepreneurs how to automate, systematize and grow a small business. Kim has trained over 30,000 entrepreneurs, and has been featured as an expert on Forbes, Fox Business News, and other media outlets.

Kim lives in Salt Lake City and frequently travels with her husband and four kids.

Made in the USA
San Bernardino, CA
04 January 2015